Radio Adventures
of the
MV Communicator

by

Paul Alexander Rusling

Published by World of Radio Ltd, Hull, HU10 7TL, UK.
Printed by Book Printing UK, Peterborough, PE2 9BF.

Although every precaution has been taken in the preparation of this book, the publisher and author assume no responsibility for errors or omissions. Neither is any liability assumed for damages resulting from the use of information contained herein.

ISBN Softback   978-1-900401-12-8
ISBN Hardback   978-1-900401-14-2

CONTENTS

Part 1 The Mouth of the Thames

Part 2 The Mouth of the Thames

Part 3 Scuppered in Scapa Flow

The 11 radio stations which broadcast from the ship are

LASER 730
LASER 558
LASER HOT HITS
RADIO SUNK

HOLLAND FM
HOLLAND HOT HITS
HOT HITS 1224
VERONICA HOT HITS
Q RADIO
Q THE BEAT

SUPER STATION

21 years of fun packed excitement

All the stories in this book are believed to be true and every attempt has been made to verify them with those present at the time. Some information has been omitted to protect individuals. The Communicator operated at all times within the law and no laws were broken by the ship operating on the high seas, or within Dutch or British Waters; all applicable licences were always obtained.

Advice relating to the legality of offshore broadcasting, in particular the Marine Offences Act of 1967, and various telecommunications and broadcasting legislation of the United Kingdom and the Netherlands is given in good faith but professional advice (see page 203) should always be sought by intending broadcasters.

by Paul Alexander Rusling

To my lovely wife Anne,
"My Soul and Inspiration"
without whom this book would never be finished!
and to my children Dawn and Ben
and my Granddaughter Verity

and to my many former colleagues
who gave their life and soul
for the eleven radio stations that
broadcast from the MV Communicator

ACKNOWLEDGEMENTS

I would like to extend my gratitude to the many who broadcast from the radio ship MV Communicator and especially to those who gave their permission to disclose information or provided assistance in putting this book together. Two gentlemen without whom the project wouldn't have happened are John Kenning and his friend Phillip Smyth. They didn't play an operational role, but they were essential to the project starting; they can both be proud of what they began.

The Communicator stations owe a huge debt to some excellent engineers: first Blake Williams without whom the project would have finished in the early days and secondly to Chief Engineer Joe Vogel who became so ill through work on the ship that sadly he paid 'the ultimate price' in May 1989. Others too, of particular note José van Groningen, Mike Barrington and Dennis Jason, as well as the many who kept the Communicator's eleven radio stations on the air.

There were so many who played a role in the stations on the Communicator, that I should have fitted a revolving door on the ship! Among the key people who played leading roles in different phases of the ship's 21 year broadcasting career are Nick Murray, Ray Anderson, Fred Bolland, Nico Volker, Unico Glorie, Peter Jansen, Rob van der Vegt and Dave Miller. Theirs are not the big star names that listeners will recognise but they each led teams whose work gave the Communicator such a long and high profile radio career.

I am particularly grateful for help and additional information to Hans Knot, Blake Williams, Mike Barrington, Dennis Jason, Herbert Visser, Ruud Poeze, Chris Edwards, Ben Bode and my former colleagues in NOZEMA. More historical details on some of the stations can be found in the essays on the *HansKnot.com* web site. More detailed biographical information about many of the disc jockeys heard from the ship can be found on: *www.offshoreradio.co.uk*, and on *www.offshoreechos.com*, whose work has been very useful to cross check many of the details in the book.

Thanks are also due to those who have allowed photographs to be used in the book, especially the Hans Knot Media Archive, Leendert Vingerling, Dennis Jason, Peter Harmsen, Luuk Meuwese, Chris Edwards, Dave Chappell, Gary Markham, the many individuals who held my own camera for pictures on so many occasions.

Paul A. Rusling
October 2016

Part 1 – The Mouth of the Thames

1. BROADCASTING FROM A SHIP

A radio station on board a ship; it sounds an odd idea to say the least, especially one wildly rocking far out at sea! That might sound to the layman one of the strangest places on earth to broadcast from. Dangerously high voltages, seawater and ever-seasick disc jockeys all make for quite a potent mixture. So why broadcast radio programmes from a ship?

The reason goes back to the very dawn of broadcasting, in the 1920s. Governments all over the world were anxious to control this new media and they imposed tight rules on who could and who may not broadcast as well as the material that might be discussed on the air. The lightest regulatory touch was that of the FCC in the USA, but even they were quite strict about things like power levels, and programme material. Broadcasting was subject to the law of the land, which demanded licensing and that was controlled by governments.

Government laws however only control what happens on their sovereign territory and in a narrow strip of sea along their coast. That strip of territorial waters was, for many years, three miles. The measure was chosen as it was about the distance a cannonball would travel, at the time when the first international agreements about 'territorial waters' were made, and it's been that way ever since. A few countries claim wider strip as their own and those claims are generally respected, though not universally accepted.

In recent years UNCLOS (United Nations Convention on Law of the Sea) extended territorial waters to twelve miles, with a further area of up to 24 miles to protect some nations' areas of economic interest, a so-called 'contiguous zone'. Even further out to sea, an area called the adjacent continental shelf extends to two hundred miles from a country's shoreline. While countries may exercise some rights out to two hundred miles offshore, here the area gets quite muddy, especially as far as protecting radio spectrum goes.

The two hundred miles limit brings a lot of countries into conflict and has not been 'tested', i.e. no country has tried to exercise its right to control ships, and especially not to board any for either checks or to impose its domestic laws, on ships so far from its coast.

Not all countries accept the UNCLOS regulations and several have so far refused to sign. Most European countries including the UK ratified the treaties eventually, but many countries do not accept the UNCLOS conventions, including Israel, Syria, Turkey and the United States.

Out beyond the limits of territorial waters is an area that is not within anyone's territorial waters is known as 'the high seas' that by international agreement belongs to no one. These 'international waters' were agreed to enable the ships of all countries to pass unhindered between neighbouring states. They are sacrosanct and well defined in international treaties. Fishing, oil exploration and travel are all vital to the integrity of 'international waters' and it is very rare for a country to interfere with the peaceful passage of another nation's ships, except in times of war. Indeed, the act of aggression on another nation's ships has often been an act of war and precipitated lengthy disputes.

During the years of prohibition, organised crime syndicates in the USA realised that operating on boats located just outside territorial waters was a great way to get round many laws, particularly the lucrative vices of gambling and drinking. Offshore casinos with licensed bars popped up off California and to promote their services they established radio stations on board.

Among the biggest of the ships were the *City of Panama*, which broadcast its own station on 815kHz AM, and a ship called *Rex*. They were run by mobster Tony Cornero and financed by Bugsy Siegal, a legendary underworld figure at the time. They spent over $1m US to equip and float their ships, whose radio signals could be heard all along the western seaboard of the USA, attracting business to the ship. With a staff of 300 it could hold over 2000 customers, so clearly the offshore gambling boats were a big business. Without the radio stations on board them, it's doubtful they could have attracted enough business.

Harassing the supply boats ferrying customers out to the ships did not work on the biggest operators so the Attorney General of California, Earl Warren organised a small flotilla of official boats and set off for the biggest ship. The officials were repelled with high-pressure fire hoses but the siege continued for nine days, while the gangsters patrolled the decks with sub machine guns. Eventually Cornero's men surrendered and the battle switched to the courts, where they were fined.

A year later the courts ruled that the three mile limit for territorial waters would be extended to encompass the entire Santa Monica bay, thus driving any ships far out to sea, too far to make the trip attractive to gamblers. Without the gambling trade the ship's radio stations closed down, as the stations were only on the air to carry adverts for enterprises that shore based stations were not allowed to broadcast.

by Paul Alexander Rusling

The idea of extending territorial water by drawing a 'bay closing line' across wide inlets is an interesting one, used again in the UK in the sixties. The shoreline's low water mark (called the baseline, from which all territorial limits are measured) can be drawn across the mouth of an indentation, where the volume of water within the artificial line is greater than that covered by a semicircle drawn with the line as its diameter. Generally countries simply use a 24 miles long line as the baseline, the maximum permissible under the UNCLOS treaties.

This practice was adopted by the UK in 1964 and it decided the selection of the anchorages chosen for many radio ships ever since. It was also a key tool used by the prosecution in cases against radio broadcasters using abandoned military structures out in the Thames estuary. Justifiable for security reasons, it has been exploited in various areas, such as by Libya at the end of the 20th Century when they applied it to the 'bay' of Benghazi. An international dispute over territorial waters between Malta, Libya and Tunisia had to be decided by the International Court of Justice in The Hague.

High Power 'Border Blasters'

By the 1930s it became possible for radio stations to cover much greater distances thanks to newer high power transmitters. The American FCC put a cap on the power levels of stations, which encouraged local broadcasting, with a few large networks developing, such as NBC, CBS, Mutual, etc.

Those limits of power output did not apply over the border in Mexico and several entrepreneurs set up very powerful stations, with power levels up to 250,000 watts, five times what was permitted in the USA. These cross-border stations did good business running commercials for products that were banned from the airwaves in the USA, including several medical services of dubious efficacy, such as goat gland transplants for 'gentlemen of diminishing libido'.

Some stations thrived for decades, especially those in Tijuana who could reach across into California, and others further east with large audiences across in Texas. After dark, the nature of Medium Waves meant that such stations were heard all over the USA. In the 50s and 60s, some stations acquired legendary status, with Wolfman Jack becoming so famous.

A blockbuster movie, *American Graffiti, was* built around his programmes. Directed by George Lucas it created a mysterious aura around the Wolfman, located just over the border. In reality, Wolfman Jack was heard on several stations in Mexico, including the giant XERF station whose massive 250,000 watt signal could be heard right across North America after dark.

Wolfman Jack's growling and exuberant style was exciting to kids seeking something different; it was rebellious and somehow just a little bit 'naughty'. He adopted mannerisms and phrases used by black artists and for some years he kept his ethnicity secret, believing that by sounding as if he might be black would attract more of the young white kids, which is just what the advertisers wanted.

Wolf knew exactly what the kids wanted to hear and talked up his own mysterious persona on the air, giving an illusion that the border blaster stations were somehow not at quite mainstream and 'your parents wouldn't approve'. That was a huge part of the appeal of such stations to young American kids from the late 1950s until the late 1970s.

By then Wolf had moved to syndicating his shows over a hundred stations all over the world, from Los Angeles. He also became a well known TV star but always kept that cloak of being somehow just on the wrong side of respectable, which he recognised was the main draw to his youthful audience, many of whom were now becoming the much sought after 'Baby Boomer' generation.

In Europe it was the young audiences that most radio stations that broadcast from the radio ship Communicator sought to reach, as these are the audience most desirable to advertisers. These are targets for many advertisers, being the ones who have not yet developed brand loyalties. They are the most vulnerable switching by radio campaigns.

Radio broadcasting in the UK was swiftly harnessed by the Government who prohibited any non-BBC broadcasts. No private radio broadcasting was licensed at all until the 1970s, partly due to left wing politicians hating any form of enterprise and governments in general simply wanting to control everything.

The BBC's institutional empire was run by a dour old Scott called John Reith, whose strict Presbyterian upbringing did not permit such frivolous things as music and other forms of entertainment. This was especially so on Sundays, when the BBC broadcast lots of church services and hymns and very highbrow material.

It wasn't long before entrepreneurs looked to setting up set up private radio stations just outside British waters. The Daily Mail newspaper acquired a ship to beam radio entertainment into the UK around 1930, however technical difficulties defeated them. They resorted to using loudspeakers on a boat, anchored off the UK's popular beaches and broadcast audibly. There were many complaints once the initial curiosity had died down and the experiments stopped.

Across the English channel, countries like France had more liberal broadcasting regulations and gave licences for commercial stations. Most of these continental stations broadcast light music and entertaining quizzes, all paid for by advertisements interspersed around the programme items. The big ones had transmitters in Paris, Luxembourg and a variety of other countries.

Radio Normandy began in 1925 and beamed signals from its transmitter at Fecamp (in the Benedictine liqueur distillery) on the northern coast of France. It had prestigious offices in London, right opposite the BBC and was run by the International Broadcasting Company (IBC) whose MD Leonard Plugge later became Member of Parliament for Chatham. Radio Normandy had excellent reception over southern England.

The station aired only popular programmes and of course many national commercials. Its most popular shows were talent competitions, recorded in towns all over the UK.

In those days before tape, the shows were recorded directly onto huge 16-inch diameter shellac discs and then shipped out to the transmitter in northern France for broadcast. Sometimes they arrived late or even broken, so the presenters had to ad lib programmes. They were in effect the first 'disc jockeys'.

Plugge made several reconnaissance trips across Europe checking reception and signing up other radio stations to broadcast the IBC programmes. A weekly publication, *Radio Pictorial*, gave all the tuning details of the stations, which continued to mushroom until the outbreak of WWII. At that stage most closed, and the rest were taken over by the Germans, who used the transmitters of the largest one, Radio Luxembourg, for their own propaganda.

After World War II, the NATO countries wanted to spread the word of freedom behind the Iron Curtain that had descended across Europe. Much had been learned in the war years about the value of propaganda, especially by radio. Once the Cold War began in the early 1950s, the three main powers stepped up their international transmissions accordingly.

Some of the western broadcasters, such as the BBC *World Service* and the USA's *Voice of America,* could not be clearly heard in many parts of the USSR, so the American coastguard took a leaf from the mobsters' book and fitted out a ship called The Courier to beam its radio programmes into Russia. The best location for the ship was found to be at the eastern end of the Mediterranean Sea, from where the MV Courier beamed in its diet of news and comment.

USCG vessel W410 'The Courier' with MW balloon antenna

The VoA ship had very powerful medium wave and short wave transmitters on board, over 150,000 watts, very high power levels for that period. Most of the programmes were originated at studios in the USA and sent to the Courier by short wave radio. Technicians on the ship recorded them and then rebroadcast them on the on board MW and SW transmitters.

Several antennas were installed on the ship, including a novel long wire antenna held up by a helium balloon floating several hundred feet above the deck. This was an excellent way to get the most efficient (electrically) aerial on a ship out at sea. The reason for this is that a medium wave antenna needs to be very long if it is to operate with reasonable efficiency. The operation was a great success and the ship only stopped broadcasting when the Greek Government gave the Voice of America a permanent base in Rhodes in the mid sixties.

by Paul Alexander Rusling

Almost every Government in Europe kept very tight state control over broadcasting; almost all the private stations that had been tolerated in the 1930s in some countries, were frozen out after WWII. Some entrepreneurs thought the *Voice of America* ship in the Mediterranean was a good template for setting up stations in Northern Europe and by 1958 the first stations were heard in Scandinavia. They were a success, and Radio Mercur was swiftly followed by *Radio Syd, Radio Nord* and many others.

Word of this method of circumventing broadcasting legislation, by going offshore, spread to Holland and Belgium and then eventually the UK, with the first radio ship off England being *Radio Caroline* in 1964. She arrived just in time to help boost the British music explosion, spearheaded by the Beatles and the Rolling Stones. In the mid 1960s over a dozen stations were beaming the latest music into the UK from a variety of ships and former defensive forts.

Most of the stations were starved out by new legislation in 1967 by the Marine Offences Act, which made it an offence to use a British ship for broadcasting in British waters, to supply anything for use in offshore radio. For the first time it became illegal to play a pop record, read the news or preach a sermon on the radio, if it was transmitted by a ship at sea.

Radio Caroline bravely continued, obtaining supplies from Holland, which had no such laws until 1974. In that year, the Dutch brought in similar legislation and three of the four radio ships moored off its coast, Radio Veronica, Radio Atlantis and Radio North Sea International, all closed down. Radio Caroline again continued and moved its remaining ship, the MV Mi Amigo, to a convenient anchorage just off the Thames estuary from where the station could be well heard in London, as well as in France, Belgium and Holland.

No one seriously complained about Radio Caroline and so little enforcement action was taken against her. Eventually in March 1980 the ship ran aground on a sandbank in the Thames estuary, and was lost. The Radio Caroline family promised to return, but few thought the station would ever reappear.

The following year, a new station called *Radio Paradijs* challenged the Dutch Government's anti radio ship legislation. Within days their ship was seized by police and navy commandos and the ship towed into Amsterdam, where it remained for many years while owners fought the government in court.

The real reason for the prolonged incarceration, chained up in the harbour, was to win compensation from the Dutch Government, largely over action of raiding or seizing a ship while it was in international waters. That seemed to quench whatever thoughts some parties had for launching another radio ship in the North Sea. The owners of Radio Paradijs were astute businessmen led by Ben Bode and were eventually awarded far more in compensation for the arrest of their ship than they had ever hoped to make from operating it!

Ben Bode, one of the owners of Radio Paradijs, pointed out in 2016, "just think of all the money we saved on fuel and wages while our radio station was not on the air!" Sometimes it is indeed more profitable to not operate. Some years earlier Radio North Sea, a Swiss owned radio ship, earned almost two million Dutch guilders by agreeing to silence their transmitters, with the silence paid for by one of their competitors, Radio Veronica!

It made commercial sense to them as the brash and noisy RNI operation antagonised the Dutch authorities and gave them cause to outlaw offshore broadcasting. Buying the silence of a competitor cost only a couple of million guilders, but enabled Radio Veronica to continue their own operation, said to be worth almost 10 million a year.

Broadcasting from a ship – it is indeed a very strange business!

LEGALITY

It is still possible to broadcast radio programmes from a ship at sea but professional help is recommended to circumvent the legislation and technical difficulties. Huge audiences can still to be reached in many places and its not necessary to be a lottery winner to accomplish it. Seriously intending and financially qualified operators are advised to contact the broadcast consultancy on 199 of this book for assistance. We do not advise anyone to break any laws and strongly urge anyone considering this exciting way of broadcasting to engage professional help. While it's true that hiring professionals can be expensive, it is doubly true that amateurs will invariably cost a lot more!

2. AN IRISHMAN'S TOY

Meanwhile, in Ireland many radio entrepreneurs had discovered that it was possible to simply set up a radio station on dry land without a licence. The authorities were pretty impotent to act, only able to levy a simple fine of £15 per day for operating a radio station. Small beer, when some of the stations were making more than that per hour!

The Irish radio scene mushroomed until the early 1980s, by when there were several large well-run stations attracting more listeners than any of the state run RTE services. The leader of the pack was undoubtedly *Sunshine Radio*, run by former Radio Caroline DJ Robbie Dale. Robbie brought his former shipmate Spangles Maldoon, into the fold who, under his real name of Chris Cary, would soon become something of a broadcast entrepreneur.

After realising how wide open the Irish market was, Cary decided to break away from Sunshine and launch his own station, which he did in 1981. The station was called Radio Nova and it broadcast with a stronger signal than any other on the FM band. It was an instant success and soon added MW and even LW transmissions that could be heard across the UK.

To get the station off the ground, Cary offered shares via his accountant, including to a Dublin hotel owner called Philip Smyth. He promised that his new station would soon be a huge success and probably have millions of listeners. Cary invariably acted very quickly and soon had Radio Nova up and running. The station was a huge success, and did indeed attract millions of listeners in Ireland and on the western side of the UK.

By 1982 Radio Nova had around half the total radio audience in Ireland and launched a second station called Kiss FM to cope with the huge level of the advertising revenue it was now attracting. Plans for a Nova TV service were also underway as well as more powerful equipment to reach into the UK. The Nova brand was often the subject of the headlines in every newspaper in Ireland; it had huge public awareness and, for the most part, support.

Realising that his procrastination had caused him to "miss the boat" Smyth decided to act a bit quicker next time such an opportunity came around. Just a few months later such an opportunity arose; while on holiday in Les Arc, a skiing resort in the Alps, he was chatting to Neil Ffrench Blake, a former executive at Radio 210, the local commercial station in Reading, Berkshire.

Neil was working on several secret radio stations on behalf of both the British Foreign Office and the USA's Central Intelligence Agency. He noted Smyth's interest in radio and introduced him to a young disc jockey called John Kenning who was keen to discuss some ideas to replace the void left by the loss of Radio Caroline. John had some innovative ideas, including calling the station 'Lazar' (sic) and having futuristic sound effects such as those from the Star Wars movies, including the sounds of 'laser blasts'.

Smyth was curious about the idea of a radio station on board a ship and rather fancied the idea of having one in Dublin Bay, that could at times be sailed down to Tramore, a holiday resort on the south coast of Ireland, where he had summer home. He discussed the idea with one of his advisers, Roger Parry, who was a journalist at the BBC. Parry's colleagues at the BBC gave more helpful advice and several meetings were held at the Dorchester Hotel in London.

Parry recommended that Kenning get some assistance from *Broadcast* magazine, a weekly glossy trade newspaper. The magazine's editor recommended that Kenning approach Paul Rusling for help; they had been in touch many times as both were committed radio enthusiasts and Rusling had advised *Broadcast* on technical matters from time to time.

Rusling and Kenning got on famously, at least initially, and were soon enthusiastically swapping ideas for the proposed station. Both were still somewhat in awe of an American owned Top 40 station, *Swinging Radio England* that had briefly broadcast to the UK in 1966, seventeen years previously. Rusling and his wife were regular visitors to the USA and radio stations. He had recordings of '*Boss Radio - SRE*" which he played in his car, mixed with more recent presentations of Wolfman Jack. Both Rusling and Kenning were both were very keen on the idea of having a radio station broadcast a Top 40 format using American DJs to the UK.

It had originally been suggested that no advertising be accepted, as the owner would pay all the operating costs. Paul implored John to ensure that the radio station had a credible sales office, able to generate enough revenue to keep sufficient revenue streams to the station afloat.

Within ten days, the pair were on a flight to the USA, where they met with several of Rusling's contacts in the advertising world. The most receptive to the project was Roy Lindau, a time broker at *Major Market Radio*, a company owned by Gene Autry. He had been involved with the abortive attempts to refloat Radio Caroline the previous year and was very impressed at some aspects of the plans that Kenning and Rusling produced for the new station.

Roy Lindau had been vice-president at Major Market Radio for ten years, before which he sold time for Westinghouse in New York and Chicago. He claimed to already have potential advertisers for the project who he described as "very easy, a total pushover." He said he was confident of being able to book around $1.5 million worth of advertising in the station's first year, rising to around $4million a year.

The figures that Lindau proferred made a lot of sense. Rusling's costings had suggested they needed about £350,000 to set up and around a tenth that every month in recurring operational expenses. If even a fraction of Roy Lindau's forecasts could be achieved, the project looked like being very profitable.

"The key to getting the advertising would be to have a high profile presence here on Madison Avenue," explained Roy, reeling off a list of the best known agencies and other support companies in the advertising industry who were all clustered around the mid-Manhattan thoroughfare. Roy spoke incessantly of a concept he called pan-European advertising, an idea that unfortunately eluded most time buyers in radio.

Most multinational companies have separate marketing departments in each territory, usually a single country. They each like their own budget and to make their own arrangements. Media outlets in European countries are so disparate that it doesn't make sense for countries to meddle in buying even in adjacent countries. It was to be some time before anyone in the organisation realised how nebulous the concept of pan-European advertising was, a discovery that was made the hard way. Roy had been just as upbeat about his expectations for Radio Caroline two years previously. "Buying airtime with us is perfectly legal and it's the only way to reach the whole country at this price," he told the New York press corps. "Besides, deep down, everyone wants to be a pirate."

Roy Lindau in the Madison Avenue office.

Over dinner that night in New York, Lindau confided to Rusling that he had left Radio Caroline after almost $2 million went missing, somewhere between the investors and the station's office, and that it had all been in cash! He also said that a team of mobsters had got involved in the Caroline relaunch and he roundly dismissed Radio Caroline's founder, Ronan O'Rahilly, as "a total flake" who could not be trusted.

Rusling had known O'Rahilly for many years; indeed, he had first met him while still at school and he regarded him as one of his radio heroes. Rusling became instantly wary of the slick talking New Yorker, but was at the same time impressed with his knowledge of radio sales. Only much later was he to become aware just how treacherous Lindau really was and how his prowess was not in 'selling' radio air time at all, but simply in the clerical process of booking air time on radio stations.

The UK's Marine Offences Act made it an offence to supply or equip a radio ship while in British waters, so it had been decided to fit the ship out in the USA, where such laws did not apply. Rusling and Kenning met with Martin Cooper from a company called *Transcom Inc*, a Philadelphia based equipment broker who supply new and used equipment from a variety of suppliers.

Martin has a wealth of radio and TV expertise and is one of those likable 'can do' people. He offered to consolidate all the necessary kit into one place and arrange for the ship to be fitted out. Originally this was to be in Philadelphia, however the port was later switched to Port Everglades, as it would be close to the largest items to be supplied, the transmitters.

Building the necessary transmitters within the time schedule John was demanding would be quite a call. Rusling knew that the latest transmitters were expensive, at least six figures. They often had complex circuitry that could lead to problems at sea. Radio Caroline and some other offshore radio stations had obtained some transmitters in 'used' condition but these could often have problems due to age and were difficult to arrange spares for, especially out in International Waters.

The solution was to have a new transmitter that uses 'old school' tried and tested technology; a company called CSI Transmitters Inc had just the right units. They had solid anode modulation based on principles that were simple and straightforward. Most importantly, they could be obtained at a price that wouldn't break the bank. Martin knew the owner of CSI well and flew with Rusling and Kenning down to his factory in Florida to introduce them to him.

CSI Transmitters had been established at a base near Philadelphia but the Gellmans had recently relocated their team to Florida for the better climate, and to be closer to the Central and South American markets where they sold many FM and AM transmitters. The new factory was a large modern building housing metal fabrication and assembly lines with about a dozen staff. The transmitters were all built into two tone brown and beige cabinets, or "coffee and cream" as Bernie's daughter Robina called them.

Rusling forged an instant bond with the owner of the CSI transmitter company, Bernie Gelman, that was to last for many years. They discussed other options for operating radio stations in Europe and vowed to work on other projects in a similar vein.

Bernie was fascinated to hear about the *Voice of Peace*, a radio ship operating off the coast of Israel. His family was Jewish and he and his wife said they would like to help the *Voice of Peace* and supply it with new and more powerful transmitters, and at cost price!

The pair of CSI AM Transmitters on the MV Communicator

3. THE GARDLINE SEEKER

In March 1983 John Kenning and Rusling travelled to see several ships at various harbours and ports around the UK and it was on a trip to Aberdeen that they first saw the Gardline Seeker. The ship was owned by Gardline Shipping of Lowestoft, a firm headed by George Darling. The name Gardline is an anagram of the family name, with the letter 'e' added.

George was a descendant of a legendary heroine, Grace Darling, whose father was a lighthouse keeper in Northumberland. In one fearful storm in September 1838 she had rowed an open 21-foot open boat and helped to rescue 9 crew and passengers from the Hull to Dundee paddle steamer, the Forfarshire. It had foundered on the rocks during the night and 53 souls perished.

Grace and her father were awarded Silver Medals by the *Royal Society for the Preservation of Life* (now called the RNLI) and over £700 was raised for her by public subscription, including a £50 donation from Queen Victoria. Grace died in Alnwick of tuberculosis aged only 26 and the poet William Wordsworth wrote one of his best-known works about her the following year.

Lighthouse keeper's daughter Grace Darling to the rescue

There is now a museum in Bamburgh dedicated to Grace's achievements, and folk singer Dave Cousins of the Strawbs wrote a love song to her for his album 'Ghosts'. There have been many books, plays and musicals featuring Grace's story, but her greatest legacy is that the RNLI now use her image as their figurehead, in recognition of the works that Grace performed after the rescue, to galvanise support for the society in its formative years.

After spending all morning measuring every nook and cranny of the Gardline Seeker, Rusling agreed that a radio station could be accommodated within the ship, with some modifications and additional equipment. John Kenning said he would put the wheels in motion for a quick purchase.

The Gardline Seeker had been working as a marine geophysical survey ship, carrying out offshore geotechnical services off the Scottish coast. This work was primarily undertaken for the Admiralty, making charts and some seabed research work.

She was equipped with extensive scientific laboratories at the stern of the ship and a bespoke anchor handling system in the bows. The huge 'A' frame and chain rollers were ideal for deep-sea mooring, which would remain at sea for long periods.

**John Kenning with a picture of the ship
in the Aberdeen office at first inspection**

The vessel also had comfortable cabins for up to twenty-three crew and other staff, making her well-suited as a radio station. Her upper cargo deck contained a couple of modular buildings with exercise equipment and other recreational devices for the crew and scientists, which could be useful for the crew and a full complement of radio station personnel. The gym area was retained and expanded; it became popular with most of the Communicator's crew and team of DJs over the years.

The Gardline Seeker was the type of cargo ship, or freighter, called a 'tweendecker,' with the hold space divided horizontally by decks. This plan drawn at the start of the conversion work shows how the two decks were divided to accommodate equipment. The top deck was divided vertically across the ship to form a for'ard generator space, to keep the noise and vibration as far away from the crew accommodation as possible. The transmitters were close to the generators, to avoid long power cable runs, but still quite accessible to the aft end of the ship, with a large extractor above for cooling and a feed through insulator for the output to the antenna.

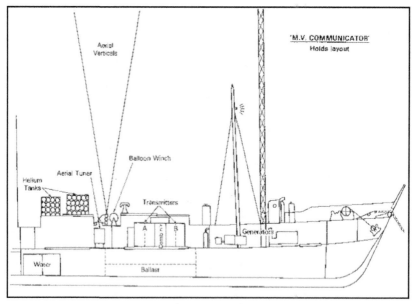

Deck area section

The for'ard end of the upper deck was converted into a generator room for extra electrical power. Three 50Hz AC generators had been installed already, to run scientific equipment and provide 'domestic' supplies to the cabins in her years as a survey vessel. This ticked yet another box; in the early 1980s many ships still did not have an AC supply for the cabins, just a lot of equipment running from a DC supply, which often created difficulties. There have been many problems on ships and even accidents arising from inexperienced crew and passengers plugging in equipment not designed for DC operation.

An area of well over a thousand square feet and eight feet high was available which would be more than adequate for high power AM radio transmitters. There were serviceable hatches and provision for ventilation and RF signal output onto the deck area where the antenna would have to be installed.

The lower deck had several ballast boxes, containing about 100 tons of sand, which helped the ship sit well in the water, as can be seen in the General Arrangement plan below.

Ballast tanks could be used for trimming the ship as her fuel tanks became progressively emptied by the thirsty diesel generators. She had a total capacity of 73 tons of fuel (over 17,500 gallons, or 81,000 litres). This was likely to be more than sufficient for around two months continuous running at full power. A further 6 double bottom bilge tanks could be used for carrying extra fuel.

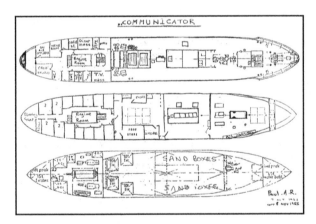

General Arrangement (deck plans)

On the flight back to London, they discussed the type of equipment that would be needed for the ship and whether it would fit into available holds. Rusling had measured these carefully and advised Kenning against using old, used equipment due to its inherent unreliability, but also because older equipment tended to be up to 8 feet high. Equipment so tall could not be easily accommodated in the limited headroom available. Newer broadcast transmitters tend to be a lot shorter, needing only about six feet of headroom, and would fit more easily into the Gardline Seeker.

Suddenly, work on the project seemed to stall; no equipment was ordered, the ship purchase was called off, none of the staff previously discussed had been taken on and Roy Lindau cancelled his London trip. At Easter, Rusling met with the founder of Radio Caroline, Ronan O'Rahilly, as had become an annual tradition. He tried hard to convince Rusling that there wasn't really any money in John Kenning's project and that he was being 'played along' by someone's mind games.

Not long after the inspection of the ship Paul Rusling left the project after being told by his contacts that none of the transmitter equipment, which required long build times and needed properly scheduling, had been paid for. Even the promised deposits on the ship and the equipment had not materialised.

John Kenning was increasingly unavailable and when he did surface he was invariably too busy for ship talk as he was starting a land based pirate station called *Radio Sovereign*. It was to be an 'all gold' music station, serving the area around his home in Twickenham. Rusling assumed the offshore project using the Gardline Seeker had died and forgot about the project.

MV Communicator in the 1970s as the MV Charterer

It was to be three months later that Rusling unexpectedly had a call from another former Radio Caroline executive, **Paul Hodge**. He assured him that the project was certainly going ahead and asked him if he would re-join the team. Rusling agreed, so long as his bills were settled. Hodge immediately visited Rusling at his Whitstable pub, the Punch Tavern, and paid him a month's salary in advance, if he could start work immediately. Hodge disclosed that Kenning had left the project and was busy running his own station in London.

Later that week Hodge and Rusling visited the head office of Gardline Shipping in Lowestoft, where over £60,000 in cash was handed over to the somewhat bemused owners for their ship the Gardline Seeker. Sale documentation was handled by a form of marine lawyers, *Ivan Cohen & Co* of Geneva, Switzerland and the buyer was *Deka Overseas Ltd*, a company specially established to own it. The 'Deka' name had been a spur of the moment flash of inspiration by Rusling and Hodge to be a tribute to their favourite British record company, Decca; it was almost named Tamla Motown!

Once the £60,000 deposit had been paid for the ship, stores were quickly loaded. The Gardline Seeker was ordered to sail immediately to Port Everglades in Florida, where she was to be converted for her new role as a floating radio station. The nine man British crew sailed the ship out into the eye of a Force 9 gale and headed south, through the Channel and out into the Atlantic, destination Florida. Port Everglades had been chosen to fit out the ship, as it was the closest to the factory building the transmitters – CSI Electronics in Boca Raton.

The following week Hodge and Rusling met with Lindau and another project executive called Len Muller in upstate New York where the main aspects of the project were agreed, with the owner participating by long distance telephone call. The name of the station was agreed to be Laser and its format would have an American sound similar to *Swinging Radio England*, a station that both Rusling and Kenning had fallen in love with back in their schooldays. The station would use a revolutionary kind of 'linear tracking' turntable which enabled records to be played at any angle, but that idea was soon dropped in favour of committing all the music to NAB cartridges.

Over the next week several office suites were viewed, including some in the World Trade Centre and others in the Panam Building. Eventually a suite of swish offices at 341 Madison Avenue was chosen. Muller and Lindau were adamant that a location here was essential, as the street was the centre of the advertising industry and they believed this alone would precipitate orders. Liincdau had used exactly the same lure when selling his firm to sell for Radio Caroline two years before to Vincent Monsey and Anthony Kramer.

Roy, his wife and an assistant went shopping for furniture and restaurant accounts in which to entertain prospective advertisers, while newly appointed Chief DJ **Rick Harris** hit the streets to buy material for the station's record library which were then shipped down to the base in Florida. He also ordered the latest production items (short audio recordings) from the leading suppliers: *Valentino's, Cheap Radio Thrills, LA Air Force*, etc.

The latter is one of the best-known radio production houses, and features recordings of Phil Music and his Tijuana Pit Band, Dorkapellas, Audio Pro's and similar musical magic assembled by Dan O'Day. They had also marketed radio sound effects called *Laser Trax* produced by the late Terry Moss in Los Angeles in 1979, but were yet unheard of in the UK at that time. Those products were to be heard often on Laser 558 and indeed provided the mainstay of the station in its early years

The best-known items however were the laser gun effects which Rick decided were perfect for the station. He was absolutely right and the ones used on Laser were much used by other stations in Europe for the next twenty years. It was a great salutation to an inspired idea, that had been originally proposed by John Kenning in his very earliest plans for the station, back in the early part of the year.

The ship arrived off Port Everglades at 8am, precisely the time her Captain had calculated three weeks earlier in Lowestoft. Her crew reported no problems on the crossing and Gardline's Chief Engineer, John Clarke, spent two days writing up detailed notes for the ship's next crew on how to operate her.

Rusling and Hodge were by now armed with a new flag and papers renaming her *Communicator*, along with a registration certificate showing her new home was in Panama. The name Communicator seemed so apt and it was to survive her 21-year career as a radio station.

Being staffed by Americans the Brits immediately began referring to her as The MV Percolator and later, when it was heard she had females on board, some would unfairly call her the MV Fornicator. Most personnel however stuck to the golden rule of "no relationships while on board the ship" . . although not everyone!

Once a ceremonial raising of the flag had been performed and her health toasted in Champagne (we drank it, rather than broke the bottle on her bows) she was taken into dry dock at Tracor Marine Inc, to have her bottom scraped, a fresh coat of International Orange paint applied and her anodes replaced.

She also had long copper plates attached to her keel to enable better ground conductivity, which made excellent connection with the sea water, the best way to get a strong signal from an offshore radio station.

Port Everglades is a large port used mainly by cruise liners, situated just south of Fort Lauderdale, a half hour drive from Miami. With three or four flights a day to London it also had excellent connections to the rest of the USA and the Caribbean. The Tracor Marine shipyard was well equipped with everything needed to put the new radio ship into excellent order for her new role. Several huge floating dry docks were available and it was onto one of these that the Communicator was sailed to have the work done.

Two full surveys were arranged with ABS (American Bureau of Shipping) and Germanischer Lloyd to ensure the ship would always be insured and her registration easily accepted. This entailed having an $11,000 US fire fighting system installed, as well as new hatch coamings to ensure the watertight integrity was intact.

Two new 'Detroit Diesels' generators were being installed to power two new 50-kilowatt transmitters, each comprising a pair of a T25 *CSI Electronics* transmitters. One station was to be owned by the original Irish backer for the Laser project and the second station would be owned by a syndicate of equipment suppliers from nearby Boca Raton and Philadelphia.

The rest of the ship was subjected to a thorough cleaning and any defective items were replaced, with no expense spared. A plinth for the satellite dome was built on the stern deck to house a £35,000 steerable satellite dish, another first for an offshore radio station.

The satellite installation was intended to keep the radio station personnel on board in constant touch with the New York office, primarily for commercial traffic.

Telex and telephony lines were also available through the satellite link, the first time such communications had been used on an offshore radio station.

While the engineering work was going ahead, Chief DJ Rick Harris was busy interviewing prospective DJs for the station. An advert in Radio & Records had brought hundreds of applications from DJs from all over the USA, several dozen of whom were flown to Florida for interview. The first qualification was that they must be single; a good policy, as long tours of duty became normal and it avoided the problem of spouses demand regular payments of salary.

The DJ team in their Communicator 'K' T-Shirts in Florida.
Steve Masters (the first one), Jessie Brandon, Joe Vogel,
Commander Buzz Cody, Rick Harris and Dave Lee Stone

It had been decided that only American DJs would be hired, for legal reasons. As US citizens on board a Panamanian ship in International Waters they would not be subjected to the UK's Marine Offences Act, if the ship was also supplied from a country that had no similar legislation, such as Spain. In those circumstances no offence would be committed and the station could claim it was a completely lawful operation, breaking no laws.

Eight disc jockeys were hired initially plus two engineers and they were all accommodated on an entire floor at the Breakers Hotel, on Sunrise Boulevard in Fort Lauderdale. Some studio equipment had been installed in some of the rooms and several thousand empty cartridge shells and some lubricated tape obtained.

Using cartridges was an excellent idea as these were easier to use than vinyl records, especially if the weather was very rough. The main advantage however was that the music would always sound as fresh as the day it was transcvribed as there would be no cue burn or other vinyl artefacts to be heard in the station's output. The station's record library and news operation were being refined and staff trained using a *KayPro 4* computer, another 'first' for an offshore radio station.

NAB audio cartridges

Rick got his team busy loading the cartridges, ready for the music to be added. The empty cartridges needed various lengths of the endless tape loops inserting, and it was an excellent way to 'bond' the team together. Indeed, one DJ, Melinda was going to use Melinda Bond as her 'on air' name at first, but later she chose the name **Melinda Clair**. Unfortunately Melinda was destined to leave The Communicator before the station launched, which was a big shame as all that heard her 'dry runs' agreed that she would have been a very popular DJ.

The long DJ meetings were amazing sessions with exhuberant DJs, all high on soft drinks and inane radio chatter, the biggest anoraks ever! They were all of a similar age and eager for the adventure about to unfold.

Rusling and Hodge's role in Port Everglades was to each oversee aspects of the ship's conversion and refitting from an office at the Tracor Marine shipyard. The DJs spent their time winding carts and spinning tales of radio, in between sunbathing, beach games and babysitting the Rusling's daughter Dawn, now almost a year old.

Blake Williams & Melinda

29

As the Communicator approached completion the backers of the second station got increasingly concerned at the lack of firm commercials being booked. Following three days intense meetings in New York it was announced that the second channel would not be going ahead after all, only one station would now broadcast from the ship. The second consortium from Boca Raton had lost confidence in the New York Sales operation and they had their equipment removed from the ship.

This change in plans caused one of the key engineers to leave – he had worked for three or four days solid with very little sleep to get the equipment installed and was then asked to remove the third and fourth transmitter units – the final generator was still on the quayside when the 'abort' command was given. He quit on the spot, and refused a $5,000 apology to stay.

That left the station with only one radio engineer, in the form of **Joe Vogel** who had been lured away from a local AM FM combi' in Fort Lauderdale, WEXY and WAXY. He was not comfortable with high power AM but had a crash course in the 'care and feeding of transmitters' at the CSI factory with Paul Rusling and was assured that he would get a couple of deputies as soon as possible. Joe was the oldest on the team, and a first class DJ (as Mighty Joe Young), although he was rarely heard on the air as he was always busy with transmitter work.

Paul and Anne Rusling take the helm of the Communicator

The Balloons

No extra masts were fitted as it was intended to use inflatable dirigibles (balloons) to hold up the 354 feet long aerial wire that had been guaranteed by their supplier, *Raven Industries* of Sioux Falls. CSI's Chief Engineer, Jim Pinkham, had flown these successfully from a ship in his US Navy days. The radio station's engineers were taken down to a remote US Air Force base in the Florida Keys early in November. At Cudjoe Key they were shown two of the devices, flying at around 900 feet high

Underneath the balloons above Cudjoe was a gondola containing a generator, which powered powerful radar transmitters, to watch for drug runners crossing the Caribbean. They also beamed three channels of TV programmes to Cuba, about 80 miles away. Their latest balloon was called Fat Albert and was deisgned for 10,000 feet. The manufacturers and two US Air Force specialists assured the radio station's engineers that the Communicator's blimp would be fine at 350 feet. Fortunately a spare one was bought, "just in case".

The radio team for the Communicator was slowly growing in number, although many more DJs were interviewed than were actually hired. One of Roy Lindau's pals, Scott Randall, was detailed to taking care of the DJ team and help them acquire music libraries. One vital task the DJs had to accomplish was to complete reams of paperwork to obtain a passport. Like the majority of Americans, some had never travelled outside the USA and had no passport.

Scott had worked in several creative industries and was married to an artist. He had a film team make dozens of photographs of the DJs and ship while in Port Everglades; they also made a short promotional video which had been slated for showing on MTV however their launch in Europe was continually put back and it was decided to sell the footage as a VHS tape on the radio station. Scott was later responsible for the station eventually getting a Managing Director who knew quite a bit about running a radio station, although sadly that event was not to be for another year, when his wife introduced John Catlett.

Before she sailed, the Communicator had to jump through quite a number of hoops, though not physically of course! All her equipment had to be thoroughly checked and proved to meet the latest SOLAS requirements, her watertight integrity had to be checked at every point, which involved directing fire hoses into some odd places and going behind with blotting paper, that changed colour if water was getting through. A fire hose was directed onto the ship's plates during the soak tests.

The surveyor also wanted to see the broadcast transmitters running, although he was not qualified in electronics and Paul Rusling had to explain what their many meters all meant. Finally a bundle of certificates was issued covering everything, from de-ratting, through the ship's lifeboat radio equipment, to the air conditioning plant!

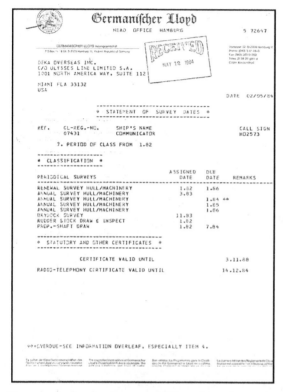

The Communicator, looked very smart, when she finally said on the 15th November. She made a steady nine knots and her engineers; Jack Meisner and Bill Voigt reported that all was running perfectly.

The Captain put into the Azores ten days later to take on further stores and a little RnR for the crew. The DJs were mostly enjoying their cruise to Europe, even though the captain insisted they take their turn at watch keeping. Two of the radio team, including radio engineer Joe Vogel were terribly ill during the voyage.

After leaving the Azores the ship then headed north, bound not to the North Sea but for New Ross in Ireland. Some additional equipment was loaded here, including an extra generator that Paul Hodge had finally got agreement for. It was waiting at the quayside with Paul Rusling and one of the promised extra engineers, Blake Williams, a DJ and engineer from Phoenix, Arizona.

Local customs officials from nearby Waterford were happy to go along with the story that the ship was still carrying on its oceanographic research. They signed off the ship's manifest after hearing how the large cabinets in the hold (the transmitters) were special computers for tracking jellyfish, which might lead prospectors to oil deposits under the sea bed. Two local newspapers ran lengthy stories about how this ship berthed in New Ross harbour was going to change the face of oil exploration.

Unfortunately, New York had issued a Press Release when the ship sailed, and given an interview on Radio Netherlands weekly 'Media Network' programme. It gave all the details of the Communicator and new station. As a result, quite a gathering of radio enthusiasts assembled on the New Ross quayside to greet the ship when she arrived. The attendance of Paul Rusling with an extra generator on board convinced them that this was the ship enthusiasts all over Europe were awaiting.

There was considerable debate as to why the station was to be called Laser. The name, albeit spelt differently, had been one of John Kenning's original plans for the project, based around the sounds of laser blasts he wanted to feature. It also made it sound slightly futuristic, the laser only having been invented about twenty years before. The tight focusing of the programming and laser light was also very apt.

Some executives of the Ford Motor Corporation encouraged this, with promises of advertising if the name 'Laser'; could be turned into a buzz word with young 'boy racers.' They were launching the *Laser Capri* in the UK, although the name had already been used in Australia for over a year. During the early discussions with Ford and their advertising executives, someone asked if Ford were worried about what the British Government might think: "Hell no, we don't worry about what the US Government think, so we're not gonna lose any sleep over the British Government!" was the response.

The original DJ crew on the poop deck of the Communicator

While the ship was in New Ross, the project's owner drove down from Dublin to have another look at his million dollar toy and a temporary aerial was rigged so that a selection of his favourite music could be transmitted for him to hear. At last the DJs could play some music, but they spent most of their spare time in New

Ross exploring, some saw the nearby Kennedy homestead, the SS Dunbrody emigrant ship and of course the *Dunbody Inn*. If the DJ's weren't in there, then you could usually find them in *Prendergasts*, right next door!

After being cooped up on the ship for the three week Atlantic crossing (except for a few days in the Azores) they just wanted to get off and onto dry land. New faces made a nice change too. As healthy young Americans they were all concerned to exercise every day – Steve Masters loved skipping and, when the deck stayed horizontal, would spend a lot of time up on what later became known as 'Splinter Beach'.

After a week or so in New Ross the interest in the Communicator and its all-American crew became a bit too intense and the decision was taken to put to sea again to sail the final two hundred miles to the Thames estuary.

Steve Masters exercising on deck

The voyage around the south coast of England was not a comfortable one with a Force 9 gale once again blowing up the English Channel – it took three hours just to round Lands End. The only drama during that voyage however was ashore, as yet another key man resigned from the team.

Paul Hodge, who had been the key organiser, had now lost all confidence in the New York 'front' management. After lengthy phone calls with the owner and New York, Hodge called Paul Rusling to say he was resigning. He said he was not willing to risk his liberty with the project and advised Rusling to do the same. It was a very difficult time, with the extra pressure of a busy pub to run, not to mention a little baby girl at home. Underneath however, ran a deep desire to do more to help the Laser project. Some of the crew had become close friends, after working with them for so many months in Florida building the station.

The ship anchored in the Thames Estuary just before Christmas and Captain Bouchier decided to drop anchor just one mile from the shore at Margate. No one had any instructions or knew what to do next and the New York office had simply closed down for Christmas and New Year holidays.

A team of specialists had been booked to attend the ship and launch the balloons but they never showed up, so Captain Bouchier and his Chief Engineer Jack Meisner set about starting construction of an emergency aerial to be used, pending the balloon experts' arrival. Rusling was told that the balloon experts had been cancelled to save their fees of $6,000.

Captain Bouchier and First Mate Meisner

With Hodge having departed, Rusling was asked to go to the ship and supervise the launch of the balloon to get the station operational. It seemed reasonable to do this last task as there was unlikely to be any official action before the ship started making any transmissions. The authorities were also thought to be unlikely to be working over the Christmas holiday, so Rusling took the risk.

Late on Tuesday 27th December a tip off came that the DTI had chartered a boat for the following day to go and visit the Communciator, and it was to be accompanied by the Kent police boat and a Customs launch from Dover. Rusling immediately thought back to the day eight years ago when another radio ship had been 'visited' in the Edinbrughs (A channel a few miles away from Margate in the Thames estuary) and the Captain and three crew members arrested. The Communciator was clearly in British territorial waters (Margate roads) and might meet the same fate.

Rusling made some arrangements to have mooring specialises meet the Communicator later that day out in the Knock Deep channel, and at 2 am he set off from Margate harbour in a small launch. Visibility was less than a hundred yards, however on reaching the Communicator her Captain refused to move. Even when told that the authorities could be on their way to visit the ship he wanted to remain there until he had firm orders from New York by Telex. The crew were roused and ready to go, the engine was running, but still he wanted to think about it for a few hours. After some heated discussions and several satellite phone calls the ship the Captain eventually relented after Rusling threatened to fire him with immediate effect.

Within minutes the Communicator was underway to the safety of international waters and a rendezvous with an anchor handling tug in the Knock Deep channel. An eight-ton anchor system was quickly arranged on the seabed, comprising a huge 5 ton concrete sinker block, an 'Admiralty pattern' anchor weighing in at half a ton and about 160 shackles of heavyweight chain.

The Communicator was securely moored later that day, just two miles south of the Radio Caroline ship, the Ross Revenge. Her position was confirmed by Decca Navigator using Loran C and the satellite phone system, as

51° 39' 25" North,   01° 31' 30" East

This location was known to be not only outside the three mile limit of British Territorial waters, but also outside the 'bay closing line' which had previously been used to snare the unwary, who thought the limits were measured only from the low water mark, or extended by sandbanks. Part of the Knock Deep was even beyond the 12-mile limit however this was in the process of being amended. Radio Caroline had anchored its ships in this stretch of water for almost ten years without any intervention by the UK authorities. It was safely out of the recognised shipping lanes and just beyond the view of the PLA's radar scanner at Warden Point on the Isle of Sheppey.

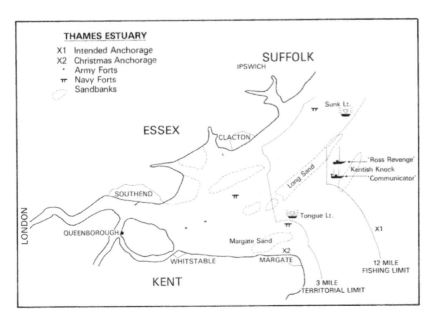

With the station's main organiser having resigned, the next problem was to organise a supply chain, as Paul Hodge had taken all the details with him and was holding them until his pay was released. Rather than pay Paul Hodge his due salary, Roy Lindau demanded that Rusling organised fresh supplies. There was also the satellite's gyro system to be fully adjusted and new regulators obtained for one of the generators, plus fresh supplies, all by a company with no credit or even any presence in the UK.

Fortunately Rusling had his pub' business to fall back on and was able to organise the heavy capital items and supply runs to the ship. At £600 a trip they were very expensive however there was considerable extra 'security' in using a professional firm and their very experienced seaman. Van rentals, bulk supplies of fresh meat and vegetables and customs duties on items which New York suddenly decided "absolutely had to be sent to the Communicator" all added to the bill.

It was decided get all the matters completed before broadcasts commenced, hoping there would be no action from the authorities to halt support from the UK. Rusling gave succour to the crew of the Communicator, who had felt abandoned with no apparent interest from their New York HQ. As well as providing essential supplies from his pub at Whitstable using a Kent tug company, he also had to escort key helpers from British Telecom, Marconi and even the BBC, out to the ship to complete jobs.

The Marine Offences Act was legally a 'grey' area; for the most part being untested in the courts, especially for a new radio ship not yet on the air.

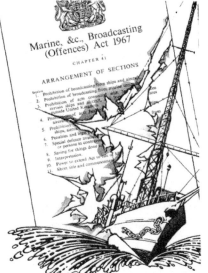

Providing equipment to a ship known to be intending to make transmissions is one thing, and arguably in breach of the Marine Offences Act. Providing "succour and support" however seemed to fall through one of the many loopholes. Many things were necessary to secure a conviction; the station had to be broadcasting, the 'offender' had to know they were flouting the law, they had to be caught in the act and prosecuted within two years. In addition there were defences such as assisting a crew who were ill, in danger or difficulties.

4. LASER 730 – FLYING HIGH

By the third week in January the ship was ready to launch the balloon and start transmissions. The weather looked kindest for Saturday 21st January, a crisp clear night with not too many isobars, indicating a period of relative calm. Late on the Friday evening the platform on which to inflate the balloon nudged her way down stream and out into the Thames Estuary. That 'platform' was a coaster, the Jostrica, a large Panamanian cargo ship. She was a bit larger than the Communicator itself, and had a large clear deck area midships and level hatches, ideal for assisting with the balloon launch. After tying up alongside the radio ship, one of the TRF (Tethered Rigid Fin) dirigibles was carefully passed across from the Communicator.

Well before dawn that Saturday morning, it was carefully nursed into life by the ships crew and the entire staff of DJs. The envelope was slowly and carefully inflated with helium, from a cluster of tanks welded to the radio ship's deck. Many couldn't resist the urge to swallow a squirt of the gas and it was comical to hear normally butch American DJs squeaking like cartoon characters at 5am!

The entire ship's company of crew and disc jockeys had to be used on deck to hold on to the tether lines and provide support to ensure that the balloon did not blow away in the wind before it was securely tethered to the radio ship. The operation was directed by the new ship's Captain, David Irvine, a former US Navy man, who had just joined the Communicator two weeks previously.

Stage One: Filling the balloon's envelope

The balloon steadily filled up and slowly rose into the sky, with tether lines and aerial carefully arranged underneath. Fully inflated she was about the size of a double decker bus and surprisingly light. Eventually it was at the correct height and Rusling was given the command to switch on the transmitters.

He was accompanied by Martin Gilbert, a British Telecom engineer from the international telecommunications station at Rugby, to assist. The engineers applied first low power, of around 12 kilowatts, and then 25 kilowatts. The antenna loaded up perfectly while Transmitter B was pumping away into the dummy load, ready for the final doubling in power to 50 kilowatts.

The DJs were by now all assembled in the studios at the aft end of the ship, almost bursting with anticipation. They were instructed to feed programme from the studios – non-stop Beatles music, which had been a tradition in offshore radio since the earliest days of Radio Caroline. This time the first track played was especially for the station's owner who was anxiously listening in London. He had by now had just spent over $1 million on this project, so the obvious choice was "Baby You're a Rich Man", the B side of their hit "All You Need is Love."

A few quick calls to contacts on shore confirmed the signal was getting out very well, everything was humming along well and Rusling was running through final check in the transmitter hall when the generators noticeably changed tone and the transmitters automatically shut down. Simultaneously a sinister metallic "whack' noise was heard above deck. Clearly, something was amiss!

Racing up to the main deck the crew found that the antenna cable had fallen across the deck, and the balloon was nowhere in sight! Most of the antenna cable was hanging over the side of the ship into the sea. It was pulled in and at the very top were a couple of clips where the antenna cable was secured to the balloon. The Kevlar connections were badly burned; they had clearly been subject to a lot of heat. This must have been caused by corona, which is an electric effect found at the high voltage ends of antennas.

The euphoria of just a few minutes previously rapidly evaporated as we helplessly scanned the skies for the balloon, of which there was no sight. It was later found to have fallen to earth about 25 miles away in Essex.

Balloon prior to lift-off, being held down by crew.

An urgent post mortem was held but it was clear that the high RF voltages at the top of the aerial had caused corona sparking. This had led to the Kevlar link between the antenna and the balloon ropes burning through just enough to let the buffeting and tugging from the wind tear it free. Both melting and tearing were present on the bits that were retrieved.

No one wanted to hang around to fly the second balloon, least of all the captain of the launch platform who had moved away from being laid 'alongside' in case they were noticed by the Air Sea rescue craft that flew from nearby RAF Manston and were frequent visitors over the Estuary. It was a pretty subdued team who sailed away from the Communicator that day, to make plans to get the second chance right.

It was simple to dissipate the corona, which is frequently a big problem with aerials. A corona shield would need to be placed at the very top of the antenna, beneath the balloon lines. Rusling devised an improved layout of the cables and spent some time over the next few days discussing the matter with the engineers at the balloon suppliers, with Jim Pinkham at CSI and with John H Mullaney, a radio-engineering consultant who had a wealth of experience with high power radio stations.

John had been developed an antenna system for Radio Nord in 1960 on the ship Mi Amigo (later used by Radio Caroline, on which Rusling had also worked). Mullaney had patented a broadband system while working for *Multitronics Inc* and was now running an independent consultancy with his son (John J Mullaney). John senior was by then in his sixties but he had lost none of his enthusiasm for radio, especially from ships.

John had also invented the now commonly found 'Folded Unipole' antenna, a form of which was used on nearby Radio Caroline, and was one of the first engineers to use computerised antenna modelling, as early as 1973. John was ready to fly over immediately to the UK and help, however New York vetoed his further involvement on cost grounds. He gave a lot of encouragement nonetheless and coached Rusling extensively on the phone.

Launch of the second balloon was set for the following Friday evening, but the winds were too strong and it was early Saturday before they subsided sufficiently. When semi-inflated and at low altitudes, the craft requires careful handling to prevent it crashing into the superstructure of the ship and its masts. Once aloft it flies stably and is steerable, by the Phillystran tether lines. (A dirigible is so named after the French verb "dirig" to steer).

During the helium fill the Communicator was approached by Radio Caroline's tender, and their manager Stevie Lane. They must have been surprised to be the first to witness the difficult birth of broadcasting from the ship. Stevie asked to come on board but the Captain refused as it was a very delicate time and it was feared they could recognise Rusling and his British engineers, now hiding below. It was important that the 'all American' story be maintained to protect the stations claim to be legal.

This time a large corona shield had been inserted between the antenna cable and the balloon and, seemingly in no time at all, the balloon was up. Power from the transmitters was applied – the full 50 Kilowatts. A visual inspection of the balloon connections using binoculars showed no arcing or sparking and its motion was quite steady, especially compared to the motion of the ship.

The usual calls to various contacts on shore were made: Herne Bay, Central London, Northampton, Manchester and Hull where good clear signals were being heard. The best surprise was that Rusling's friend Håkan Widensted at the Swedish Broadcasting Corporation in Horby was hearing a good clear signal.

Second balloon: ready and eager to fly and bring Laser 730 to life

41

**Young Paul Rusling makes the first ID on Laser
(wearing an anorak, naturally!)**

Suitably elated, Rusling made a quick station identification as everyone else was afraid of doing so, and then scrambled over the side to waiting balloon platform to head back into England. He and his team of assistants, which included experienced radio engineer Robin Banks, stood on the deck of the Jostrica, watching the balloon for almost ten miles and photographing the spectacle.

They toasted the transmissions with hot mugs of tea, high on the adrenalin of the successful launch. They knew that this was a key point in the history of offshore radio and were delighted to be part of it. They didn't realise that that the sight of the balloon was something almost no one else would ever see.

It was a surreal feeling, seeing balloon number two flying steadily at 360 feet above the pitching radio ship, securely anchored below. Even more satisfying was hearing the near vertical 354 feet aerial cable pumping out the non stop Beatles tracks played out by the DJs and knowing that the signals were being heard over much of western Europe.

No more announcements were made that day as Lindau had forbidden it, but for most of the team, just hearing the non-stop music blasting out was reward enough.

The tests on 729 kHz continued well into the evening, with non-stop music and the reception reports continued to flood in. Most were very complimentary about the superb audio quality and robustness of the signal. Even after dark there was little fading, although conditions at sea were not good – the wind having whipped round to a Northerly whole gale and also bringing flurries of snow.

As they received the reports relayed back from Laser's shore based contacts, shore, the crew and DJs on the Communicator feasted on a special celebratory dinner before turning in, many of them had been up for 24 hours continuously. They wouldn't have noticed the snow flurries turn into a blizzard after 10pm.

Finally on the air, with the second balloon.

Those members of the Communicator crew who did get off to sleep were rudely awaked during the night when the generator changed pitch as the transmitters cut out. The equipment had sensed that the aerial cable was again in the sea, and the second balloon had now gone AWOL.

Inspection revealed the break to be very low down, only 10 metres above deck. This time the antenna cable had been fed through a doughnut shaped insulator between the two ship's masts and now this had caused severe attrition, with the antenna cable fraying and eventually parting. In their haste the crew had left the four main tethering wires off altogether and secured the balloon directly onto the antenna cable with shortened Phillystran tethers. The tether cables would have held on to the balloon, which could then have been retracted and reused.

Tether cables of the Phillystran brand have tremendous strength as they use Kevlar, Twaron and Vectran in their manufacture. These liquid crystal polymers (LCP) have a high thermal stability figure, are transparent to radio frequency waves, and are almost immune to ultra violet light. Of even more importance, they are impervious to seawater, so long as the ends containing fine strands are correctly terminated; usually they are potted in metal connectors with a military grade resin compound.

The antenna cable, though many times thicker, was an alloy of copper and steel and although it was half an inch thick and looked quite strong, it was nowhere near as resilient as the Phillystran used for the tether cables. Once badly chafed in the Kevlar doughnut spacing ring, the constant tugging caused by the uplift and the wind buffeting soon snapped it. Off sped the second balloon; this time the northwesterly blizzard took it as far as Belgium.

The messages sent ashore at first light were received with incredulity. No one could believe that the second balloon had also been lost so quickly and for such a simple reason: by rushing the launch process and ignoring the instructions.

An urgent meeting at the Dorchester Hotel in the West end of London was held on the Tuesday of that week at which the future of the project was discussed. Due to the huge cost (just over $20,000 each) it was decided that no replacement balloons would be bought at this stage, despite the Communicator having nine months supply of gas on board. This was stored in two huge clusters of tanks on top of the hatch cover, mid ships.

Aerial feed (left) and helium tanks

Rusling was instructed to bring off anyone from the ship that wanted a break while new aerial arrangements could be made. On arriving at the Communicator late in evening, the crew were briefed on the prospects for the immediate future. It was likely to take some weeks to erect a practical aerial system, one that was sufficiently robust enough to work on the wild and angry North Sea. It was not going to be easy erecting sufficiently high enough masts to hold a reasonable aerial system aloft.

All but one American said they wanted to leave the ship, with only Blake Williams volunteered to remain and try and get something on the air. Most of the crew had been on board for ten weeks continuously and in the most appalling weather. Even the new captain, David Irvine, who had joined just a few weeks before, was keen to abandon ship and he told the crew that he believed the project must now be over.

With the dark and dubious news about the station's immediate future, Rusling had anticipated a mass exodus so had come prepared. The departing ship's Captain was replaced with **David Black-Davison**, a suitably qualified master from Whitstable, who was a regular customer at Rusling's pub in Whitstable. He was assisted by **Johnny Lewis,** a friend of Paul Rusling who had recently returned from Ireland and was due to join Radio Caroline the following month. Also part of the 'scratch' team, was Robin Banks, another former Radio Caroline engineer and DJ and old friend of Rusling.

It may have been contrived, or just coincidental, that all five remaining on board were engineers, but it was certainly fortuitous. They immediately set about erecting a temporary antenna using the existing ship's masts, while Rusling's contacts arranged for the airline tickets and other welfare needs of the American DJs and crew. After landing at an industrial facility in the Isle of Sheppey they American DJs and crew who had left the Communicator were met there by a fleet of cars arranged from customers at the Punch Tavern. They were then driven fifty miles across Kent to Dover, where HM Customs and Immigration could formally process them into England. This was partly for the convenience of the officials but mainly to avoid any obvious paper trail of the port being used by the Laser and her support workers.

"I don't actually know who these guys are, we are just helping them out by bringing them here for clearance," protested the driver to the Head of Customs in Dover. She was desperately trying to convince the officials that she had no idea where these illegal immigrants had suddenly appeared from, so early on a Sunday morning on the normally quiet north coast of Kent.

"Of course you are" said the Immigration Officer. "By the way, has there been any sign of that balloon yet?" he enquired. Like most officials, he knew all about the ship and was supportive of radio ships. Many of his colleagues were to prove very helpful in the ensuing months at keeping the Communicator's crew out of trouble.

Over the ensuing ten days a variety of different antenna configurations were tried, using the existing ship's masts on the Communicator. These were only forty feet high and not really suitable for a decent aerial even at the top of the Medium Wave band, much less the centre. Due to the damp conditions and unsuitably short lengths of antenna that could be raised, feeding this 'aerial arrangement' resulted in some lovely but potentially lethal and quite fiery displays of electricity in the air above the ship. Long arcing sparks danced in the air, via which you could hear the programme output.

For several days Blake Williams, Johnny Lewis, Robin Banks, Captain Dave and Paul Rusling tried to defeat the laws of physics and make an aerial that was far too short. The biggest problem was that no one knew exactly what the effect of each new change might be, so everything was pretty much 'trial and error'.

Rusling knew that there was some test equipment on the nearby Ross Revenge that would make life a lot easier and so he called Ronan O'Rahilly to get his permission to borrow it.

With the use of the neighbour's 'General Radio Impedance Bridge' all the measurements were now much more accurate. This was instrumental in enabling the team to eventually get a usable signal out. It was only a few hundred watts but it was enough to cover Essex and Kent quite well. In fact, these test transmissions on 729 kHz were heard in some surprising places. Thanks to some innovative programming by Blake Williams and Johnny Lewis, over two thousand listeners were persuaded to write in and confirm they could hear the station. This response in turn encouraged the owner of the station to stump up more money for a full antenna system.

The test transmissions were only identified as being "from the radio ship, Communicator, anchored in the international waters of the southern North Sea." At first non-stop Beatles numbers were played for a few days and then numbers by the Stones added. Finally more classic rock tracks, pop and Motown were included, along with some production beds to spice up the station ID's.

The star of the Laser 729 transmissions was **Blake Williams,** the young hireling from Arizona who had joined the station at the quayside in New Ross the previous December. He had superb production skills as well as being a great studio engineer and made the test programmes sound really slick.

Many spoof jingles and other production items from Blake's previous stations in Arizona, such as KOPA, were heard during the marathon sessions. Blake also made good use of the LA Air Force production library and the *LaserTrax* recordings.

Blake and Johnny Lewis were the only two real DJs on board. They were helped out by the Captain, David Black-Davidson, taking his turn at the panel, although he could never be persuaded to say very much.

Paul Rusling and Robin Banks had left the ship for urgent talks ashore with the owner and his lawyer, at a series of summits at the Dorchester Hotel. Young Paul Ruslings IDs in German and Dutch were heard but only as a 'pre-record' and played in from a cart machines.

Blake Williams, live on the 729 tests

It was decided to stop the 729 tests due to staff shortages and because they had proven the ship and its equipment had value. Several thousand reports from listeners had been sent to New York after two weeks low power tests which convinced the owner to invest more money for a new antenna system. It was decided to close at 4pm on the afternoon of Sunday 4th March, while there was still a good-sized audience.

The next few weeks were pretty quiet out on the radio ship and Blake grew more displeased by the treatment being meted out by Laser's lawyer and New York manager. Lindau rudely dismissed the test transmissions, on which Blake and the engineering team had worked so hard, as being "a complete waste of time." He chided Blake for daring to speak on the air without Lindau's express permission, despite the fact that his input and hard work had caused the owner to agreeing funds for a new aerial system.

The final straw came when Blake heard that the Chief DJ had vowed Blake would never be allowed to present programmes on the station again! In May Blake skipped across the street to join Radio Caroline, which he had long admired for its huge radio tower, almost 300 feet high. Blake threw himself into engineering and on air work with gusto and soon made a big difference to Caroline's output, becoming Programme Controller almost immediately.

One thing Blake did on his first day on board the Ross Revenge was to install remote start controls for the turntables. Caroline played all its music in from vinyl, the DJs had to physically hold records back and slip-start them. Difficult in a storm!

Blake Williams really became a star on Radio Caroline in summer 1984 and appears in EAP's documentary video "A Day in the Life." He was universally admired by his colleagues and listeners alike. With his bank account replenished from his work on Radio Caroline, Blake then left on a flight back to Mesa, Arizona, where his Mom kept a ranch of around 4,000 cattle.

While in Arizona Blake visited some of his former radio colleagues. One of these was Jeff Davis, who was so impressed by Blake's reports and photographs of life at sea that he resolved to try for a job on the ship as well. Jeff finally left for Europe in autumn 1985, but that's a story for a later chapter.

Blake still had wanderlust and headed off to a new life in Guam, out in the Pacific. When he returned to the States it was to the mountains of New Mexico, where he is based today. Blake still keeps his hand in the radio business, and can be heard on a couple of stations in Albuquerque. He can often be heard on *The Oasis* KOAZ, The *Cloud* 95 KKLD and on Radio Replay, a UK online station. He also performs in his own rodeo show and still finds time to appear in movies!

Andy Gemmel-Smith was a radio engineer at Essex Radio, an ILR station who was also known as disc jockey, Andy Anderson. He proposed an antenna that he promised would be 95% efficient if used on a lower frequency. He had all the details necessary to use 558 kHz AM, which had received international clearance for Essex Radio's local BBC competitor, then in the planning stages. Helping Laser to use 558, he would also help his bosses at Essex Radio.

Andy's new aerial system was a variation on the standard T aerial used on low powered local radio stations, actually an 'inverted L'. It would be held aloft by a pair of GEC lighting stanchions, 35 metres tall (about 100 feet). They are very strong as they are able to resist bending, but still have some flexibility. They slot together in sections and were delivered to a wharf in Kent where the aerial system was to be assembled, prior to being shipped out to the Communicator.

Work was commenced on adapting the masts by a team led by Captain David Irvine. The necessary stays and the cross trees were going together really well and the structure was almost ready to be taken out to the Communicator. Captain Irvine however had left detailed drawings and many incriminating papers at the hotel in Sheerness where he was staying and these had been handed in to the authorities. The Department of Trade and Industry were the arm of the British Government charged with controlling radio services and they had a small team of specialists investigating the new station. They were already closely watching the major Kent ports including Sheerness and Whitstable.

Most of those that they suspected of some involvement with the Communicator were also being tailed and their telephones were tapped by British Telecom. Fortunately the DTI's chief investigator was a partly deaf former policeman who was seconded from the Treasury Solicitor's department. He was proficient at obtaining documents such as bank statements, and at writing 'boiler plate' statements for use in court, but not very experienced in the ways of the music industry nor the peculiar world of broadcasting. As many of the transactions were made in cash, there was not much in the way of paperwork to investigate, although the private and business bank accounts of many suspects were monitored.

The Brits who were involved with the project had developed a good technique of only referring to items, places and people very obliquely on the phone. Even if the real subjects of a conversation could be guessed, there would be no incriminating evidence in a recording to tie them in to anything illegal. Some used a phone line that was simply an extension from a neighbour's line several doors away and the number was never given out to anyone.

Communications traffic between those on shore and the radio ship were undertaken using coded messages on little used or rarely monitored frequencies. The team used split frequencies, so only one side of the message could be heard.

Paul Rusling's wife had forbidden him doing any work on the mast being built ashore as he had his Justices Licence for his pub in Whitstable to protect and a baby to consider. He and his wife had now taken a back seat.

The investigators from the Department of Trade and Industry had however seen Captain David Irvine's notes that he left at his hotel and had been watching the work on the antenna masts progress for almost a week. Overhearing a message about a planned delivery run out to the Communicator, they became alarmed and decided to take some precipitous action to thwart the Laser plans from going ahead.

One morning in the middle of March they arrived at the shipyard 'mob handed' where they found a group of men fabricating collars for mounting side supports and other fixtures for the masts. They were made from long lighting columns, of the type seen on motorways. The flanges bolted onto a foundation on the deck with twelve huge bolts. Hollow inside with thick walls they would resist the enormous stresses put on them at sea. Solid walled masts are more resilient to bending, unlike the lattice sections that were later used; those proved to be far too weak for use on a ship at sea.

The DTI requested help from the local station of the Kent police, who arrested everyone working on the structure. They apologised for doing so, but explained that the supply of a mast used for an offshore radio ship was illegal under the Marine Offences Act. Captain Irvine protested that their American lawyer had assured the crew of the radio ship that US citizens were immune from prosecution.

The two huge masts and the complex maze of guy wires were seized as evidence. This was to be something of a problem for the DTI investigators; each mast was over 100 feet long, although they were still in shorter sections for ease of transport out to the ship. Nevertheless they did prove a logistics nightmare to even move them and the help of the former Post Office engineering section had to be enlisted. They were familiar with handling telepgrahph poles and had lifting equipment. Eventually it was decided to take the mast sections to a British Telecom storage yard at Bobbing near Sittingbourne, Kent, where they languished for some years, held as evidence.

The seized mast sections languish at the BT yard near Sittingbourne

Captain Irvine had made copious notes of the work and these were to be his downfall, and the main evidence of the DTI investigators, who had about a dozen Laser team members arrested. Irvine pleaded guilty at Canterbury Magistrates Court, where the prosecution revealed that they had been keeping close watch on the ports in Kent for some weeks. Despite a lot of the prosecution's evidence, such as telephone taps, being circumstantial and simply inadmissible by law, Irvine believed the project was now "dead in the water" and wanting only to get his passport back and return to the USA, he pleaded guilty. He was fined £500 plus costs, however later when it was found that the charge had been worded icorrectly this was quashed and the fine returned. Those who fought the charges were all released.

In the early hours of April Fools Day, the skeleton crew taking care of the Communicator called the shore base to report that the main anchor chain had snapped and they were now adrift eight miles south of the regular anchorage.

"Captain Dave Black-Davidson came downstairs and in a calm voice just said: "I think this is the time we should panic," remembers Blake Williams. "He steamed her back into the Knock Deep and within a few hours we were back on station, using the reserve anchor." A disaster had been averted by Rusling ensuring capable seamen were always on hand to take care of the ship.

On land, the American Captain had been badly shaken by the raid; immediately after his court hearing, he and three of the American DJ team flew straight out to the USA and were not seen again. The loss of three of the station's star DJ names was a big blow to morale; Buzz Cody, Steve Masters and Melinda Claire all took new jobs on their return to the States, Steve did very well and landed a prime daytime shift at KITS in San Francisco, California, while Buzz went back to Illinois. Jessie Brandon and Joe Vogel stayed in the UK and hid away with friends in Kent and across the channel in Dunkirk, after New York warned that they too might be arrested.

The DTI were astonished two weeks later to find that work was going ahead on the radio ship to build a new aerial. Two further steel lattice masts were delivered to the ship under the cover of darkness. The replacements were nowhere near as strong as the solid 'lamp post' masts, but the owner was promised that the new structure would do the job. The old Phillystran tether lines for the balloon were pressed into service as guy wires; being electrically transparent, they obviated the need for most of the porcelain insulators that would ordinarilly be needed.

By May 6th the system was nearing completion and the engineers were ready to test once again, on the new frequency of 558 kHz. Only a carrier signal was broadcast at first, but the following day non-stop music began with Queen's *Radio Ga Ga* being the first track played. The power was very low, just a couple of kilowatts as the new aerial system was arcing and sparking, which the transmitter was not at all happy with!

During the process one CSI unit was cannibalised for the parts. The combiner, which added the output of the two transmitters together, was stripped of its coils and capacitors. One section of the combiner is all that now remains of the ship; it is now installed in the communications room on Sealand as a working souvenir.

Tuning coil from the CSI transmitters

New components including coils and vacuum capacitors were obtained and fitted and the bandwidth improved by widening the aerial. It took several weeks of continual adjustments to get the aerial to accept reasonable power levels. Just one transmitter could be used at half power, 12.5 kilowatts and even this meant fitting extra tuning components into the transmitters.

There were also problems with linearity and asymmetrical modulation. The transmitter the waveform had a distorted modulation envelope and adjustments were needed. Several launch dates passed including the Whit Bank holiday weekend, that was going to be the big Launch Day. It too was missed however eventually, later that week; the station was finally ready to start broadcasting.

It wasn't a moment too soon as six months had now passed since the Communicator left Port Everglades, and she had been in the The Thames Estuary for five months. Her neighbours on the Radio Caroline ship, the Ross Revenge, would frequently make sarcastic comments about the silence from the Communicator. Along with everyone else within a few hundred miles they were about to discover what was wrong with radio and what a big noise the Communicator could make.

Before sharing the excitement of the Laser launch, here is a look inside the ship, to give you a taste of life afloat and the layout on board. The living accommodation was all at the aft end of the ship, the part with superstructure. On the deck level there were two longitudinal corridors running around a central portion that formed the upper part of the ship's main engine room and the funnel. Off the starboard upper corridor was a TV mess, toilets and washrooms, and then the larger studio, mainly used for production, which was the furthest aft. At the very back was a door leading onto the poop deck, the tiny areas at the very back, above the ships rudder. Coming back up the port side was the main 'on air' studio, then newsroom, a chilled room for drinks storage and then the dining messroom where most meals were taken. Slightly for'ard of that was the galley.

Immediately outside the galley was a short corridor running across the ship which had a wide staircase (unusual on a ship) to the below cabin area. These were a mixture of doubles and singles, all panelled with wood and containing one or two bunks, a washbasin, a locker and seats. Each cabin had 240v, with UK style outlets.

Above the deck level, a stairway near the newsroom led onto the upper deck, which became known on board as Splinter Beach. On this level was a cluster of butane gas bottles on the port side for cooking along with the ship's lifeboat, at the very back was the pedestal for the satellite dish and then forward was the Captain's private cabin and dayroom.

This room was also the ship's office, where visiting officials such as Customs, pilots and the ilk would be received, or the crew carpeted! Stairs just outside led up to the wheelhouse, which had the helm, engine room telegraph and navigational equipment. The radio room behind it was equipped with MF, HF and satellite communications receivers.

Communications Room on the Communicator (by Leendert Vingerling)

5. LASER 558 – THE LAUNCH

On Thursday the 24th May, without any fanfare or advance notice, Rick Harris opened the station at 5am. After playing several jingles and IDs over the sound of waves crashing on a beach, he said:

"Good Morning, I'm Rick Harris, and on behalf of David Lee Stone, Jessie Brandon,
Steve Masters, Joe Young, Tim Levensaler, Bill Voigt, Dennis Lassiter, and about
four dozen other people,
I'm pleased to introduce you to a brand new radio station,
All Europe Radio, Laser 558.
Broadcasting Live from International Waters from the MV Communicator we
promise to bring you 54 minutes of hit songs each hour that we broadcast.
All the hits, all the time.
We shall also keep you informed with world news every hour.
Speaking for all of us, Welcome to Laser 558,
*where you're never more than a minute away from music, starting **now!**"*

Rick was the godson on Roy Lindau and so became one of the first people to hear about the project. He was also the first DJ that the station signed up, in August 1983. He had worked on his college radio station in Plattsburgh, New York as well as stations in Vermont and in Cape Cod, Massachusetts. Rick had a very 'laid back' style with a lower baritone voice. He was very well read and had a wide knowledge of world affairs and music.

The first four names Rick mentioned were the entire DJ line up of Rick, Jessie, and Dave, who had all made the trip across the Atlantic on the radio ship, plus a replacement Steve Masters. 'Mighty Joe Young' was the on the air name used by engineer Joe Vogel, who had his hands full with transmitter duties.

The DJs had to work five hour shifts on the air initially, something becoming normal in the USA by then but unheard of in Britain where most radio DJs were on the air for just one, two or at the most three hours.

Jessie Brandon had travelled around quite a bit as her father was in the US Military. She had an impeccable pedigree in radio, with a degree in film, journalism and in broadcasting, and had worked on 13 radio stations already.

She also spoke Russian, and had worked on most types of station, including rock, country, MOR, and had been a DJ on WOMN, a soft rock feminist station. She was one of just two females who made the crossing on the Communicator, but by launch date she was the only woman on board a ship with a crew of fifteen. She was Laser 558's first Music Director, responsible for selecting the music, especially the songs on hot rotation.

Dave Lee Stone was a former actor and model and had also been lead vocalist in a band in California. "I didn't join the project to make a fortune, I joined for some adventure and to have a good time," he told his colleagues during one of the many lengthy discussions the radio team had.

"It's a good feeling knowing that I could always go back to California and get work there at any time, but for now I'm looking to have a good time in Europe. It's somewhere I've heard a lot about and always wanted to visit," said Dave, who hosted show called "Stone Zone" and a Motown special programme which was often repeated.

"The big lure is London as so much of my favourite music comes from there and it's a place that I feel an affinity and maybe I could even fit in there for a while and get some work there. This could be the planet's biggest radio station, in one of the world's most exciting places. Who wouldn't want to be a part of this? I would probably work on the station for free I think," he confided.

The fourth DJ heard on the air after the station launched was **Steve Masters**. This was not the original Steve Masters, who had left back in February and was not broadcasting on KITS, a Hot Hits station in San Francisco. It was decided that too many changes would not look good so a former radio airtime salesman called Dan Crafton was hired to become Steve Masters. He hosted late night programmes on the station, but only stayed for a few weeks. As soon as Laser hired more DJs hired he left, to pursue a career in media consultancy in Paris.

The launch team of four DJs were joined on the air a couple of days later by **Paul Dean,** a voice who will have been familiar to many radio listeners in western Europe. Paul had worked on another radio ship, Radio North Sea International, ten years before, where he was known as Paul May. He had been born in Detroit, Michigan to a war bride who originally came from Norwich.

He was a tall guy who had lived in East Anglia for many years. This had given him a strange accent but was an American citizen who was fortunate enough to make many trips home to his Aunt's in Norfolk. While on holiday in East Anglia he heard Radio Caroline, but it was Radio London that made him decide to get into radio, which he later did at a small local radio station in Leonardtown, Maryland.

Paul Dean *(by Leendert Vingerling)*

Paul grew up listening to Canadian stations from across the border, and was an avid reader of the NME. He knew that he really wanted to be on a British station, and in 1971 when he was 21 he applied for, and got a job at Radio North Sea International. He left the ship when he got married and moved to Norwich taking a job with Norfolk Council and DJing at night.

When he joined Laser in 1984 he was told to report to Whitstable where he was put up by the station organiser in a bungalow. He was amazed to see huge bundles of cash to pay for fuel and food. It was stashed in drawers, in cupboards, in boxes, on the table, everywhere! "It was all that money lying around everywhere that convinced me they were serious and meant business."

A song that Laser did get solidly behind was *Relax* by Liverpool band 'Frankie Goes to Hollywood.' They already had their second release *Two Tribes* scheduled when Laser launched but constant plays of both propelled both into the top 2 chart positions, despite *Relax* plays on the BBC being almost non-existent.

6. SELLING THE LASER AIRTIME

As with any new radio station, the birth calls were soon heard: "Please advertise on our station" was the message as intending advertisers were invited to contact the exclusive world agents of Laser 558, Music Media International on Madison Avenue in New York. Roy Lindau was now styled company president and he courted many international advertisers that he thought would welcome the opportunity to reach the Laser audience.

This was now estimated by the BBC to be in the region of 4.5 million, although it was claimed by MMI, the station's advertising agency, as being in excess of 10 millions. There was a strong case to argue that Laser now had a couple of million listeners in the Benelux countries where the signal was particularly strong, however a reasonable estimate of this would not have been more than 7.5 million.

The coverage map being sent out by the station had not been updated to show how far the 558 coverage was reaching, but the old 729 kHz map was simply being used. The coverage of a transmitter will be different on each frequency, partly due to the propagation characteristics, but also the ability of listeners to tune to it due to co-channel users and those stations on adjacent frequencies. These all have a different effect for different frequencies.

Most advertisers would have checked with their own local offices whether the station was reaching listeners in the areas claimed, which it clearly couldn't do. While generally speaking, the lower the frequency the wider the coverage, it would be limited in some directions where there are co-channel or adjacent broadcasters. These affect reception of the desired signal in many ways. The limitations imposed by an antenna's height also mean that it might be less efficient at certain frequencies, meaning that more of the energy being pushed up it by the transmitter might be consumed in tuning and matching circuits, resulting in less signal being radiated.

A huge amount of lavish press information packs were produced and mailed to literally hundreds of prospective advertisers in North America and almost every tiny media outlet imaginable in Western Europe. The QC's legal opinion on the radio station's legality was copied to many advertisers and some were offered to have their own legal cost paid to investigate this further, something that an American lawyer was not qualified to do anyway.

Many prospective advertisers were royally treated to lavish lunches and dinners in Las Vegas and Cancun, Mexico, while Lindau flew First Class to an ever-increasing number of destinations to try and open the doors to advertisers.

The first Rate Card offered time in either 30 or 60 second spots at up to $500 per minute, which had it all been sold would have produced the station $33,000 a day, or just under $1 million every month. With costs initially running at $110,000 a month ($63,000 of that being spent at the New York and Miami offices, and less than $40,000 a month to keep the radio ship running and supplied) that would have produced a healthy profit and paid back the investment in the project very quickly.

The big problem was simply that Roy Lindau was unable to fullfil the promises he had been making for a year of around $10 milllion a year revenues; in fact he was unable to sell any advertising.

LASER·558

ALL EUROPE RADIO

Charter Rate Card One

Days	TIME SEGMENT	Classification	GRID	30 Secs	60 Secs
Mon. - Fri.	0600:0900	PEAK	1	$250	$500
			2	$230	$460
Saturday	0900:1200		3	$210	$420
Mon. - Fri.	0900:1400	PRIME	1	$200	$400
Mon. - Fri.	1630:1830				
Saturday	0700:0900		2	$190	$380
Saturday	1200:1500		3	$180	$360
Sunday	0900:1400				
Mon. - Fri.	1400:1630	A	1	$150	$300
Sunday	0800:0900		2	$140	$280
Sunday	1400:1600		3	$130	$260
Mon. - Fri.	1830:0200	B	1	$100	$200
Saturday	0600:0700		2	$ 90	$180
Saturday	1500:0200		3	$ 80	$160
Sunday	0600:0800				
Sunday	1600:0200				
Mon. - Sun.	0200:0600	C	1	$ 60	$120
			2	$ 50	$100
			3	$ 40	$ 80

All rates in U.S. dollars.
All time segments in Greenwich Mean Time.
Available to qualified multinational advertisers only.

Merchandising

Laser offered listeners free membership of The Communicator Listeners' Club, with a membership card being issued free of charge. It's a proven method of creating strong brand allegiance. It also encourages listeners to call in for dedications and to enter competitions and draws held live on the air, it developed a keen awareness of the station and the ship's name.

As well as selling airtime third parties for advertising, the station also raised substantial funds through the sale of its own branded merchandise. The usual T-shirts were offered for just £6 each, in plain white with a two-colour transfer on the front – the internationally known 'K' flag, which is maritime signalling code for "I want to communicate with you".

Also for sale were copies of a 21inches x 33 inches wide landscape poster of the DJ line up on the ship, proclaiming the first day on the air. A 15 minute long promotional video about the station that had been shot while the ship was still in Florida was also offered for sale at just £15. Badges of the Communicator's 'K' flag were issued and cassette recording with highlights of the first day on the air costing £7.

**Laser 558's initial line up of disc jockeys in the on air studio:
Jessie Brandon, Rick Harris, Paul Dean, Steve Masters and David Lee Stone.**

Within a month of launching, Laser 558 had lost its first DJ. Steve Masters (the station's second DJ to use that name) quit on the 16th June after a series of problems, meaning his colleague's shifts were extended for a few days until replacements arrived. Within a week, new DJs **Tommy Rivers** and **Holly Michaels** climbed on board the Communicator to strengthen the team.

Tommy had grown up in a mining town in northern Minnesota and joined WWTC in Minneapolis in 1976. He then moved to a small FM station and then KRSI, a big time dual AM-FM combi, where he became morning news reporter. KRSI changed to country for a few years before becoming an oldies and rock'n'roll station, so Tommy had a really good grounding in all kinds of radio in Minnesota. He answered a small display advert in the Radio and Records weekly trade paper and Roy Lindau flew over to interview him in Minneapolis. When Tommy said that the salary on offer was too low, Lindau offered to double his pay, if he would take on the role of Operations Manager.

Tommy had to fly down to meet with Glenn Kolk in his Miami law office for a complete briefing, and then spend a few days at the New York office, on Madison Avenue.

"I was so excited when I first flew over to England, about to start work on Europe's biggest radio station," he told Offshore Echos magazine. "It's every radio DJ's big dream, surely? We arrived at about 3am on a tug and it was a disappointment to find it was just a rusty old bucket; I asked myself what the hell had I let myself in for." Tommy's spare time on the Communicator was spent writing up his thesis for a degree from the University of Minnesota.

Tommy 'what a guy' Rivers in the Production Studio

At that time the programming decisions were all made by New York. All music scheduling was done from there, handled initially by Scott Randall. This was clearly not making best use of the DJs on board and was proving very difficult as the crew seemed unable to work the satellite connection and so had to use a covert VHF link to shore, suitable scrambled to mask the information.

Eventually the role of Programme Manager was given to the on board team. Initially Dave Lee Stone did Programme Manager duties but after he left to join Radio Luxembourg in 1985, Tommy Rivers took up the role.

Laser 558 had always intended to run hourly news bulletins. These were assembled in a purpose build newsroom on the port side of the ship, equipped with a British Teletext TV, a typewriter and a Kaypro computer. This was also connected to the satellite terminal, installed in the radio room behind the wheelhouse. Advertising traffic and other instructions could be sent straight to the ship from the New York head office.

The newsroom was also used by Jessie Brandon, the station's Music Director, to make up playlists to ensure the hottest hits got suitable rotation and did not come around too often. The DJs used a card index for this initially. The DJ on the air could be seen through the glass in the adjacent on the air studio, which also had clear sight lines across midships to the much larger production studio, which was on the starboard side.

The desking and many surfaces in the studios were finished in a material resembling cherry red Melamine. This was one of the latest ideas in studio design and that had been the subject of a lot of discussion and press coverage at the 1983 National Association of Broadcasters (NAB) show. Tracor Marine's contracters added the red finish to brighten the studios and to form 'easy to wipe down' surfaces when disc jockeys' lunch got 'spilled'.

DJs Paul Dean and Might Joe Young share a lifebelt

Holly Michaels demonstrates the first 'on air' mixer (Audio Technics).

Picture by Peter Harmsen

Holly Michaels was a lovely friendly lady with a soft smoky voice from Minnesota. She had trained at the prestigious *Brown College of Broadcasting*. After graduating there she joined KKBJ, a radio station near Minneapolis. In Holly's programmes on Laser 558 she was often assisted at the panel by the ship's deputy captain, Tim Levensaler.

Tim had been one of the original crew members who helped sail the Communicator over from Florida the previous November. He and Holly were to get very close over the next few months and eventually they returned to the USA and got married, though not before Holly had broken a few radio listeners' hearts, with her soft and sultry voice.

After they left Laser, Tim continued working as a ship's captain with a company called Marine Growth Ventures in Pompano Beach, just up the road from Port Everglades where he had joined the Communicator in 1983. More recently he joined a cruise line in Port Canaveral.

In a TV interview on the TVS magazine programme *Coast to Coast*, Holly told interviewer Alan Clark that "everyone on board the Communicator gets along very well, like one big happy family." She also trotted out the company line that "all our tenders come from Spain once a month so we are totally legal."

By the end of the month the fourth new recruit to the DJ team was clambering over the side, fresh in from Salt Lake City (via Heathrow and Herne Bay!) and he turned out to be the most popular DJ on Laser, **Charlie Wolf.**

The Seawolf, as he called himself, is one of radio's most outspoken radio voices. A one time Bostonian, former Jewish Mormon he had a good grounding in rock and country radio in Utah and really relished a life on the ocean waves.

Just 24 years old when he joined Laser, Charlie immediately assumed a controversial persona, who delighted listeners by poking fun at other radio stations and all forms of authority. One feature of his early programmes was ' fever pitch' where he gradually built up the tempo and excitement to 'fever pitch' before then calming things down again.

Charlie later joined Atlantic 252 and a local station in Ireland but is now heard on many BBC and private radio and TV stations. He regularly appears as a guest on Sky TV News and BBC TV reviewing newspapers and is well known for his right wing views, being a staunch member of 'Republicans Abroad'.

Charie, appeared nightly as 'The Seawolf'

At the end of the station's first month on the air, Channel 4 TV had a vox-pop poll asking people in the street if they had heard of Laser. 100% of those asked said yes they had heard of it, which was an excellent response given that the station was unable to promote itself in the UK using any of the usual platforms, TV and press advertising. Some of the national newspapers did run features about the station.

It took the New York office five weeks to send any mail out to the ship, including the DJs own personal mail although over 9,000 items of mail arrived at Laser 558's office in the first week of June. They were not ready for it and it completely overwhelmed them. In response to the big response from the Benelux, some Dutch ID's were heard on the station, the first there had been since Paul Rusling's station ID announcements in Dutch and German, back in February. The main Dutch Laser 558 ID was-

"De hits van Europa, Gooie Dag
Laser, vijf vijf acht!"

The Laser DJs introduced several new words and phrases to their listeners' vocabulary - *Splinter Beach* was the new name for the wooden deck of the Communicator, where the DJs spent many hours sunbathing, and topping up their *EuroTan 84*.

Many leading stars of the day expressed their approval, especially several new artists who had been featured heavily on the station's playlist. It was decided not to feature a Top 40 sales due to the logistics in getting accurate information, and knowing which area to survey. This was soon overturned, and Music Director Jessie Brandon added influence from the UK Top 40 as well as the Dutch chart, when the material was available.

Many stars offered to record endorsements of the station, including Paul and Linda McCartney who had excellent reception of the station at their home just outside Peasmarsh, near Rye in East Sussex. Paul had been a big radio fan ever since first hearing the Beatles first release, *Love Me Do*, on Radio Luxembourg in 1962 and Linda also seemed to have caught the radio bug. Their other main home near Campbeltown in SW Scotland was very close to Ireland, ideal for listening to the many stations broadcasting from there. They were among the first to react to the first transmissions of non-stop Beatles music: "First time I've ever heard some of those tracks on the radio, you're all doing a great job!"

"There is a big buzz hearing your songs on the radio, and knowing that so many other listeners are hearing them at too, at the same time," said Paul. He and Linda had listened avidly to the first test transmissions of Laser 730, and later to Laser 558. "We always listen in the car and around the home" was one of the many messages that Paul and Linda sent to Laser 558 by fax. At one stage the couple did consider going out by boat to see the station however their lawyer advised against it at the last minute, and the station then closed down to build a new aerial.

Paul – an early Laser lover

Many other stars were known to be Laser lovers, and not just because the station played their releases, but also because they enjoyed the Laser style of presentation and being "Never more than a minute away from music" which no other radio station in the UK was licensed to broadcast. Non stop hits, coupled with American DJs and a hint that the station was somehow just "a little bit naughty" made Laser hip, cool and trendy; essential listening!

7. LASER 558 – IT'S GETTING BETTER

During July, just six weeks after Laser launched, BBC Radio London DJ Tony Blackburn revealed in the London Evening Standard that he had invited Laser 558's very popular female DJ Jessie Brandon to stand in for him while he went on holiday.

In the article, Tony sang the praises of the new station, saying "Laser is a brilliant station, much more fun than the other pop stations. I hope its appearance will give the legal pop stations the big kick up the bum they deserve. Jessie is the best girl DJ around at the moment and the ideal person to fill in for me while I'm on holiday.' BBC bosses did not share his view however and rejected Tony's suggestion.

One of the ship's captains, Dennis Lassiter, had to be rushed to hospital in Essex by the Communicator's high-powered Zodiac inflatible after severing his finger in the main ship's anchor winch in July. His finger was severed and the wound bleeding profusely, with other crew members fearing for his life. All trips ashore were totally against New York's rules; Roy Lindau had told everyone that they would be arrested once they stepped ashore into England. He clearly had not read the legislation, the Marine Offences Act, as anyone in the radio ship business should do.

The Marine Offences Act specifically excludes mercy missions; the relevant clause clearly outlines a 'special defence' for carrying goods or persons.

> *7 (1) In any proceedings against a person for an offence*
> *it shall be a defence for him to prove –*
> > *(b) that a person on board the ship or aircraft was believed to be suffering*
> > *from hurt, injury or illness, and that the goods or persons were carried for*
> > *the purpose of securing that the necessary surgical or medical advice and*
> > *attendance were rendered to him*

It doesn't take a lawyer to understand that getting a badly injured crewman to hospital is a valid defence. Lindau must have known that; knowledge of this business was his job, but he lambasted the crew for getting the Captain urgent medical assistance. Fortunately the crew acted with compassion and the Essex police acted appropriately, and didn't press any charges.

Landing on an Essex beach the Captain was sped to hospital in a waiting ambulance that had been summoned. The hand was saved, but after a lengthy telephone tirade from Lindau over his emergency trip to a UK hospital, he never returned to the ship. No legal action was taken, even though two of those crew members on the 'mercy mission' were not carrying their passports and were technically illegal immigrants.

Back on the Communicator, the first mate, Tim Levensaler, took command of the ship and was later confirmed as the Communicator's appointed Captain. Having been with the organisation since November the previous year and helped sail her across the Atlantic, he was more than well qualified. Tim knew every nook and cranny on the ship, was a good solid and reliable worker and proved an excellent leader of the men (and girls).

Tim had been one of the more organised of the team when launching the

balloons on the Communicator. "Tim was also one of the nicest people on the ship," commented Chief Engineer Joe Vogel. "He was very considerate and really seemed to care about each individual crew members, a very considerate guy." Tim formed a close friendship with one of the female DJs who he later married. He has since gone on to a career as a passenger ship captain and a Marine Superintendant for a fleet of casino ships in Port Canaveral, Florida.

Tim Levensaler holding onto a balloon

Meanwhile, back in Florida, the Communicator was not the only project experiencing trouble with the balloons. 'Fat Albert' was aloft and working well, but getting all kinds of complaints from residents along the Keys about the noise from the generators. Being so high in the air, the noise carried a long way. In mid 1984 Fat Albert tore its cable anchors out of the ground, when it broke loose from its anchor pad during a storm. The cable tether became entangled with vehicles and had to be cut away. Fat Albert was eventually shot down by a Navy plane that tailed it for almost 200 miles.

Some time later, Fat Albert did manage to break loose again. The blimp together with 10,000 plus feet of cable headed for the mainland. Through the use of the control boxes and a chase helicopter, the US Navy was able to bleed the blimp of helium and set Fat Albert down safely in the Everglades.

In 2007 the pilot of a Cessna 182 and two passengers lost their lives when their plane flew through the restricted air zone around Fat Albert, colliding with one of the blimp's tethers. This cable held, but it sliced through the plane's wing and the aircraft crashed to the ground.

Other balloons flown from sites in Texas, in Arizona and in New Mexico, were supplied by the mighty GE (General Electric) who lost the contract after several failures. Balloons with lift of up to 13 tons have been used, but the Laser ones lifted only a quarter of a ton (500lbs), still more than enough to hoist the 150 pounds of aerial cable they were designed to hold aloft.

Today there is a chain of ten balloons flying at 10,000 feet above the Mexican border, each with radar capable of spotting planes at up to 1200 miles away. They have so far detected and tracked over 500 unidentified aircraft, most of them attempting to fly drugs into the USA.

The large blimps cost over $3million each but they have proved surprisingly resilient, except in hurricanes. One blimp was lost in Hurricane George and another in Hurricane Dennis.

It's always the tether cables that seem to fail, rather than the balloons themselves. The blimps have now become a part of the local scenery on the Keys, and indeed a part of folklore. Songs have been written about them and even roads in their local areas named after them

Back out on the North Sea, air time salesman and Road Show organiser Robbie Day was heard reading the news on Laser 558 and doing exactly the same earlier the same day on Radio Caroline – a very rare occurrence. He had always wanted to be a disc jockey on Caroline and relished the thought of being near a microphone. His sole appearance on the air was something very unusual which to his credit he managed to achieve twice on the same day!

By August 1984 Laser 558 had begun using a regular 'closedown' tune. It was one that was already quite well known, an anthem by one of the world's biggest selling pop groups, ABBA. It was the tune *"Thank you for the Music'*, which was accompanied by the following announcement:

This is All Europe Radio, Laser 558,
broadcasting live from the MV Communicator
in International Waters. Laser 558 is owned and operated by *Eurad*
***SA* in a totally free environment.**
At all times, this station endeavours to maintain standards of good
taste and responsible technical operation.

We resume our transmissions of hit music
at 5am, Greenwich Mean Time,
6am in the Central European Time zone.

Thank you for listening and have a good night.

One member of the Communicator team who did not retire at any regular time was the Chief Engineer Joe Vogel. As well as supplementing the DJ team from time to time, when he masqueraded as DJ **Mighty Joe Young**, he usually spent all night carrying out urgently needed modifications and servicing in the studios and in the transmitter room.

The right hand unit gave perpetual problems due to many of the components being plundered to change the frequency of the main unit. This caused several artefacts in other circuits and Joe spent many hours trying to rectify the problems. His clandestine radio link to a former engineer in Whitstable came in very useful at times.

The manufacturer's advice was usually ignored and the station was not given after sales support as the final bill had not been paid, nor had subsequent supplies of spare parts been paid for. Joe had to rely for advice on two previous engineers who had already left the organisation, although he was officially not allowed to contact them. Many Laser jocks were interested to learn some radio engineering and some had basic certificates, qualifying them to monitor and close down transmitters, including Rick Harris.

by Paul Alexander Rusling

Why was Laser 558 such a huge success?

There were many reasons that Laser 558 was attracting lots of listeners. In general, the programme format was something that listeners enjoyed. So let's examine what its programme format was. It could be described as simply Hit Music, and that generally is the type of format that brings most of listeners in almost every part of the world.

Many other stations however programme Hit Music, yet none was having quite the same success as Laser, and simply by 'word of mouth' advertising, as it was not allowed to promote itself in mainstream media. No other station however was playing so much hit music as Laser. The authorities helped by calling the ships 'pirates' which help give the station an aura of naughtiness, which appealed to many of its young listeners.

The station had a strict policy of "never more than a minute away from music", i.e. it did not feature lengthy talks. Almost every other station in Europe had quotas of music, which were not allowed to be broken. In the UK, the amount of music played on radio stations is strictly controlled, and limited by agreements with the copyright holders. Laser was subject to no such restrictions.

The station was not playing any commercials, which can sometimes be a major 'tune out' factor to listeners and suppress audience levels. The lack of commercials may well have helped build a big audience very quickly, although it did not help the organisation's bank balance!

Finally, British commercial stations had another 'quota' to contend with. Their regulator (the Radio Authority, as it was called at that time) had a strict rule that 50% of all airtime must be given over to what they called "meaningful speech".

The regulator was effectively 'gagging' British stations and forcing them to programme speech of a kind that listeners had demonstrated they didn't want. All simply because the regulator, with a paternalistic 'holier than thou' attitude had decreed was good for them.

Peter Baldwin, the Director of the Radio Authority had said publicly that "**It is not right to give listeners more than limited amounts of pop music, we don't think its good for them to listen to this rubbish for so long**." This was the 'John Reith' attitiude that had for too many decades pervaded the BBC and other establishment quangos. The newer commercial stations were effectively trying to fight Laser for audience share with both hands tied behind their backs!

A huge factor in Laser's success was the excellent sound quality the ship was transmitting. Depite being limited to Medium Wave, Laser sounded almost as clear as the legal FM stations on shore. Many complimented Laser on its audio fidelity saying the sound was "bright and loud'; perception is often reality and here it was scientifically true.

The audio equipment was all sourced in the USA, where AM stations use more bandwidth than in Europe. To fit in more stations, European stations are just 9kHz apart, but in the USA they are only 10kHz apart. Each gets more space to fit in the higher frequency sounds. Laser was deliberately set up to let those treble sounds through because most filters remove treble making it sound muddy. This gave Laser a big advantage, although a side effect was that British listeners on 567 kHz to the Irish RTE station experienced some interference.

 Laser played only music from tape cartridges, being recorded while the discs were still fresh and in excellent condition. Scratches were not heard on records played on Laser, they always sounded in pristine condition.

Secondly, the station used a form of audio processing that was more controllable than the better-known Optimod unit which could be quite harsh The Communicator's audio processing made by a company called **CRL;** *Circuit Research Laboratories* of Arizona. CRL's chief engineer had personally set the processors up to give perfect sound.

CRL processors on the Communicator

Thirdly, the antenna system on the Communicator had been deliberately made quite broadband, in order to stay in tune when the aerial array moved with the swaying of the ship. Normally a narrow, or 'tight Q' antenna would suppress some of the treble sounds too.

That combination of superior sound quality, a much tighter style of presentation with a bright new sound that was previously unheard in Europe (at least in recent years) with a higher proportion of the hit music that listeners said they wanted to hear. Those factors above were the main reasons why Laser 558 was such a resounding success.

Laser's success is beyond doubt, certainly for hard-core radio enthusiasts who still engage with nostaligic recreations of the station today. At the height of the station's success however it was the general public who were tuning to the station in droves. The *Media Research and Information Bureau* in London credited Laser with 4.9 million listeners by Autumn 1984.

By the end of the Summer Laser 558 was settling down into well-established programming, withbreaks for the DJs ashore, and a travelling discotheque presentation to give listeners a chance to meet the station operator. This was called the *Laser Lovers Road Show* and was run by would-be DJ Rob Day, who dressed as an American footballer with shoulder pads, helmet and faceguard. DJs on a break ashore attended and were warmly welcomed.

The latest listening figures however for Capital Radio in London were not so encouraging; they lost just over a million listeners the previous quarter and their station manager Nigel Walmsley urged the UK Government to take action against Laser. They also changed their own programme format to more closely resemble that of Laser. "If you can't beat them, join them," said Walmsley.

The ideal was for DJs to host only a single show each day, usually for four hours, although this did get stretched when the ship was short of DJs. For the rest of the day DJs could get up when they wished, have a leisurely breakfast, research some music or facts via Teletext and the books which were available on board the Communicator.

The only thing DJs were unable to do was actually communicate with their listeners or theiur family. New York had managed to lose the satellite linkand imposed ridiculous bans on visitors to the ship, even though each week around a hundred would turn up on a varity of small boats. The ship's captain had contact with the tender operator on Sheppey most of the time and Laser's Chief Engineer had contact with Paul Rusling via a covert radio link.

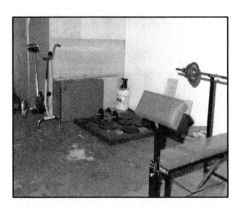

If the weather was fine they would be found sunbathing up on splinter beach, where there was also a hammock. If it was cold and wet they might head for the gym, next to the transmitter. Here they could make use of dumb-bell weights, exercise bench or an exercise bike.

DJs could always find an area of the ship to get away from their colleagues and have some quiet reflection or study for exams they planned taking.

Gymnasium area on the Communicator

8. LASER 558 – LIFTING THE LID OFF

The authorities had been concerned for some time as to who was really behind the station. The New York managers, and Roy Lindau in particular, had put out several conflicting stories, claiming that a syndicate of American investors were behind the station. A simple bit of sleuthing will have told the UK officials investigating the station that this was clearly not so, and that one lone Irishman, a quite well known resident of Dublin, was the only investor.

The Police had discovered his involvement as early as March when they raided the shipyard building the aerial masts for the ship. That raid had produced a lot of papers in the hotel room of ship's captain David Irvine, including instructions signed by "Philip Smyth, as the owner of the Communicator." Casual enquiries to many of the team soon confirmed that Smyth was in charge, and that the New York team were merely 'front men.'

That didn't really raise too many eyebrows, however the owner's coyness and Lindau's usually improbably (and often ridiculous) cover stories gave rise to further concern about what the true purpose of the station was. A straightforward commercial station could be understood but Laser clearly wasn't such a venture.

The authorities were concerned whether there could be some other purpose in spending over £1m to put a radio station at sea and generate such a huge audience. At this time terrorists were regularly attacking the UK. 1984 was the year of the closest attack the IRA had managed to make on the British Government when they bombed the Grand Hotel in Brighton where Margaret Thatcher, at that time the Prime Minister, and her cabinet were staying.

Some in the British Government suspected that the IRA might be involved in one of the radio ships, or could become involved in some way. It was unlikely to be a coincidence that both radio ships off the UK coast were Irish owned. What was their true purpose? Neither appeared to be very successful at selling commercials, despite their success at attracting large audiences. Indeed, even Radio Caroline with its disorganised way of running things had got some commercials, but Laser had none, despite its apparent professional sales team. Why was that? It was a question that perturbed politicians and Whitehall mandarins, who set about trying to discover what really was going on.

The press were also more than a little curious and set a team of journalists on trying to discover what was happening behind the scenes at Laser 558. Investigative journalist Peter Hounam spent several hours pumping Paul Rusling for information. He had by now left the organisation but was known to be unhappy that, like many others in the Laser organisation, was still owed several thousand pounds.

Rusling resolutely refused to disclose the name of the founders of the station. Others were not so reticent however and in August 1984 the London Evening Standard announced that Philip Smyth, a Dublin entrepreneur involved in businesses including launderettes, hotels and nightclubs, was the source of the funding and the sole owner of the station.

'Adviser' Roger Parry

The same article also quoted John Kenning as saying that Roger Parry, by then a well known journalist with BBC TV News, was Smyth's right hand man and had been one of the key people responsible for getting the project off the ground. He confirmed that Parry was their expert within the BBC and was often in direct personal charge of the project, as the owner's representative.

The story was a front-page splash and other media followed suit. Parry immediately protested his innocence, saying that the suggestions of his involvement in Laser 558 were 'bizarre and nonsensical.' The BBC said that if this was true then he must sue the Evening Standard for libel.

When Parry didn't go ahead with any legal proceedings to clear his name, the BBC surmised that the story must be correct and Parry was fired from his job as a high profile TV News reporter. He then moved into advertising as an executive with the London office of Clear Channel Communications. Their parent company became the largest operator of radio stations in the USA and they later became the biggest investor in a later radio station on board the Communicator (see Chapter 20, Q The Beat).

Rusling published a book at the same time, called The *Lid Off Laser 558*, which didn't go quite so far as to name either Smyth or Parry, but did give credence to the story. Rusling's book had been published to recoup over £7,000 that he was owed by the project. The book was a diary of the days setting up the radio station and dealt extensively with the equipment on board the Communciator and its conversion into a floating radio station.

Published in hardback and soft back form, it sold over 8,000 copies, in shops and by mail order. The book told the story of how the station was set up, how offshore radio stations worked, what the legal ramifications of the law were and how Laser was built. It also told of the internal problems and the many 'nights of the long knives' although it was never intended to be an exposé of Laser 558.

Paul Rusling was potentially vulnerable to prosecution under the Marine Offences Act and in August, officers from Special Branch interviewed him. Rusling's lawyer and a QC both confirmed that simply advising on installation work in the USA, in Panama and in Ireland, did not contravene the Marine Offences Act.

The police warned Rusling that his "Lid off Laser 558 book should not include the station's frequency in its title, as that might be construed to 'promote or advertise' the radio station, however no action was ever taken in the matter. Prosecutions under the Marine Offences Act must be commenced within two years of the date of any alleged offence, or they are not actionable, due to the statutory time limitations on such offences.

Section 6, clause 4, of the Act states
> *(4) .. summary proceedings for an offence under this Act may be instituted at any time within two years from the time when the offence was committed.*

The UK Government started to take what action they could against Laser and in September they lodged a formal complaint with INMARSAT, who operated the satellite that the Communicator used to stay in touch with land. The system had been flown into Miami by British Airway's freight at a cost of £9,500. The steerable aerial system for it and mount cost almost £40,000 to fabricate and install and it was costing $15 a minute for telephone calls, but had not, so far, been used to deliver a single commercial to the ship.

A lot of Laser's 'organisation' work in the UK had been carried out by a horse racing contact of the owner who lived in Newbury. John Cole was rarely in touch with the Laser team, visited the ship only once and was much older then the DJs, or indeed most of the listeners. He disappeared completely once the media began calling and he was replaced with American John Catlett.

John Catlett was a confirmed Anglophile and well travelled radio executive who had attended one of Yorkshire's leading private schools and who began his radio career aged two!

He had later worked on his university's campus radio station and he had since been business and sales manager for several stations. John had become General Manager at WBBM in Chicago, spending five years in that position. He also had similar role at WCBS in New York.

Laser 558 Manager, John Catlett

John was ideal for the role of Operations Manager because he was personable, loved working with people and loved the radio business. He was originally brought in to advise on how the station had gone so right in some ways, but was proving unsuccessful.

Catlett's prognosis was that the entire Laser organisation was simply lacking in coordination. Laser had a Marine Superintendant in the UK, a Sales Manager in New York and a Marine Attorney in Florida. All believed that they were running the whole show and none had a kind word for any of the others. What was needed was an Operations Manager, who would spend time on the ship, live within the radio station's coverage area and who understood radio advertising.

Not surprisingly, Catlett put himself forward for the job. He was ideal for the role and brought a great deal of stability to the station's UK operation at a time when they were going to need it most. One of the first things he did was get a copy of Rusling's book, *Lid off Laser 558* which, he later confided, gave him a real insight into the psyche of the station's key people, what made them tick and most of all how he could make Laser 558 more successful.

Over the next few months Laser continued to become ever more popular. Within six months, the station's audience had grown to around ten million, about half being in the UK. Many local radio stations in the station's coverage area were growing concerned at the effect Laser was having on their own dwindling audiences and of course their profits. A station for Kent, *Invicta Sound*, was particularly hard hit. Its MD, Cecilia Garnett, had given a lengthy interview to TVS, the regional ITV station for Southern England for their launch day, the first of October. Only a minute of airtime was given to Invicta Sound, while the story about Paul Rusling's book *The Lid off Laser 558* ran for seven minutes, as Laser was a subject of far greater interest than a local station.

Asked later by Offshore Echos magazine if he thought Laser could succeed today, Tommy Rivers said, "People have such a diversity of interests; videos, games, CDs and digital quality radio, its a different world now. Radio meant more in those days and it was diminishing even in the 80s. Its no longer the lightning rod on which people can get excited."

Those who had pleaded not guilty to offences during the raid on the Isle of Sheppey in the spring had their cases heard at the Crown Court in Maidstone at the end of September. Nick Murray who owned Estuary Tugs in Sheerness was cleared of supplying goods (antenna masts) to the radio ship after the prosecution offered no evidence. Rob Day, Robb Eden, John Cole, Roger Carr were charged with obtaining advertising for the station, while others were charged with conspiracy to operate an offshore radio station. It was later found that the charges had all been copied from a textbook that contained a misprint so they had to be dropped.

In October Jessie Brandon was given another compliment after the UK's biggest commercial radio station, Capital Radio, tried to copy what their BBC competitor in London had done, and offered her a job on the station. The UK Government once again stepped in and stopped Capital allowing her to broadcast from London by refusing a work permit for the Laser star. She returned to the Communicator and consolidated her position as one of the most popular and best-known radio voices on the radio dial.

Misogynists might expect that female crew members would be doing the cooking or other housekeeping tasks, but that was never the case with Laser. The girls were hired solely for their broadcasting skills and prowess on the air and it was rare for them to cook. Laser 558 always had an experienced ships cook on board to prepare meals. Originally this was Michael Dean, who occasionally was heard on the air giving culinary tips; later cooks on the ship were John and then Fiona Jeffreys while even DJ Paul Dean was very adept at handling the pans.

Fiona had often cooked on the Ross Revenge "I like cooking food almost as much as eating it," she says. "I went to Laser to help them out for a while and got paid for it, which is more than I can say about some other radio stations!"

9. LASER 558 ~ WAVES OF ATTACK

Across the Thames Estuary, *Essex Radio* in Southend was being run by Eddie Blackwell who had been a sales executive at Radio London, in the 1960s. His station was also suffering from Laser's popularity, "stealing listeners which, by rights, should be ours"he told Rusling over lunch. He tried to probe him for information, however Rusling would only offer him vague suggestion of how he might 'close Laser down'.

Blackwell assumed this meant an armed raid on the ship or something, but in reality Rusling had only one weapon, a piece of paper, which authorised him to appoint captains of the Communicator. The plan was to pay off the crew and DJs, all of whom were now owed a considerable amount for back wages not paid. Rusling could certainly have closed Laser 558, although the ship would have remained at sea and been replaced by a new radio station.

Blackwell said that he would discuss Rusling's price (£15,000) to his own bosses and be back in touch. Rather scurrilously, Blackwell had worn a radio microphone (a bug) during the interview and instructed his own engineers to record the conversation, in the hope that Rusling might give information away about the operation of Laser, which he could use to get it closed down.

What Blackwell didn't know, and what Rusling didn't tell him having suspected nothing, was that his two Essex Radio engineers (one of whom was Andy Gemmel-Smith who had designed the aerial on the Communicator) were at the time both in the pocket of Laser 558. Outrageously, they double crossed their boss and sent a copy of the illegally obtained recording to Roy Lindau. Lindau edited the recording to tell a different story and sent copies to the British media. It made a good story, that a pirate war was about to break out off the Essex coast with a takeover party being readied to "wrench control of the ship."

The real plan was to take over the Laser 558 operation armed with a few bundles of currency notes! Few newspapers gave the story any credence as it had obviously been edited and was poorly presented. When Lindau sent it to the DTI it allayed their fears that Rusling's departure was a cover. DTI investigators tried to recruit him but he remained loyal to his friends still working on the Communicator.

The 'plot' story made an interesting programme on Thames TV at prime time. Michael Wilson presented the evening *Reporting London* which spent half an hour discussing Laser and how its managers were cheating the staff. The publicity helped sell thousands of copies of of Rusling's book *The Lid Off Laser 558*.

Meanwhile the team out on the Communicator were not having such a good winter. Supplies had been allowed to dwindle and some of the food was described by the DJs as "of a far lower standard than the early days and not quite up to American standards." They were not receiving mail send from home, simply a digest of the contents of some listener mail.

One member of staff at the New York office disclosed that lots of listener mail was regularly being simply dumped in the trash as there were not enough staff to process them. Envelopes were opened and those without cheques simply discarded. That was a very harsh and unfair way to deal with listeners, the lifeblood of any radio station; especially considering the cost of airmail from Europe to the USA in 1984 was quite expensive.

The large commercials long promised were still not coming in and Roy Lindau arranged some 'contra' deals, with the USA Today newspaper and with Ski Magazine, which was edited by a close friend. These were simply trades for space in each other's publication, and not really hard sales deals. A series of trailers run on Laser 558 for a Rock Competition run by the TSB bank was exposed in a national newspperas a false advertisement, with the Bank and their co-producers the BBC saying quite resolutely that they had not asked for any commercials or other coverage on the station.

Dave Chaney was a DJ who had worked for several radio stations in California, including KLOS, KKHR and KMET as well as KOME in San Jose. He joined the same day as Der Stern, a German magazine, ran a lengthy story suggesting the Communicator was a staging ship for the distribution of cannabis plants and other drugs. The rumour may have started when visitors were excluded from some areas for no apparent reason. Der Stern also suggested the ship was run by the IRA and implicated in running guns to terrorists in the UK.

It looked like being a cold winter for Laser, Lindau's early Christmas present for the station was his resignation; he was replaced in mid December by John Moss. He was an energetic 30-year-old former advertising executive who had worked for the Radio Advertising Bureau as well as for CBS Sales and for Blair, a well-known radio 'rep house'.

In November Ronan O'Rahilly, the head of Radio Caroline, had disclosed to Dutch broadcast journalist Tom de Munck that Laser were now stealing adverts originally intended for Radio Caroline. They were doing this thanks to a spy that Laser 558 had on board the Caroline ship. He alleged that information was being passed from the Communicator straight to New York where Roy Lindau went to the client and offered free commercials if they signed with Laser. He cited one example as a recent campaign for *Rolling Stone* magazine, which Caroline had been cultivating for almost a year.

Ronan O'Rahilly and Roy Lindau were old enemies and had fallen out in a big way when Lindau had worked for Radio Caroline a couple of years previously. Roy Lindau had almost lost his secure job at Major Market Radio over work on the 'refloat Radio Caroline' project, but it ran into legal difficulties in Spain. Lindau held O'Rahilly personally responsible.

O'Rahilly had indeed warned Rusling not to even talk to Lindau at the very start of the Laser project in Spring 1983, alleging that the American had stolen a large amount of funds from the station. Lindau had similarly told quite a few untruths about O'Rahilly and Radio Caroline.

The stories began to go too far when it was rumoured that the Communicator was an offshore platform for the CIA; even the organisation's initials were present in the ship's name and in the right order too – **C**OMMUN**I**C**A**TOR.

Rumours, gossip and words untrue were the least of the ship's problems as November wore on. The flimsy aerial system sustained damage that required the help of all hands on board to get it rehung. It was just the beginning of a long-running problem that was to plague the ship for the remainder of the 1980s.

John – the cook and steward seen in Cabin Corridor.

Jessie still remembers a lot of the times on the Communicator with affection: "Most of the time we all got on very well together on the Communicator," she says. "You could always tell who had been on the ship for longest and was due for some shore leave as they would have the shortest fuse and some would blow up over the silliest little thing. In the summer it was really nice, especially on the fine days when we could go over to visit Radio Caroline. We were not supposed to even talk to them as Roy Lindau objected but, he didn't really like us talking to anyone."

Like many of the team Jessie was a little sore that the long promised advertising never appeared, nor were the crew and DJs allowed to use the satellite phone to call home, as they had been promised. "I think we only ever got one call, at Christmas in 1983," she said ruefully.

On one occasion, when making a quick getaway from a harbour, she left one of her bags behind. When it was picked up by the local police they used the contents to contact Jessie's Mum across in Maryland. They said that either Jessie or her colleagues could collect it at the police station, but Lindau warned against this saying it would be a trick and she could be arrested. In reality this help was due to a key Laser representative in that area being a senior member of the same Masonic lodge as many of the policemen and customs officers, who could usually be relied on to turn a blind eye to help the radio ships.

At the end of November Capital Radio came up with another way to get Jessie to leave Laser and join their schedule. To try and get round the prohibition on her work permit, Jessie flew to New York with Tony Hale, Capital Radio's Head of Music.

Jessie's later shows were produced by Jon Myer who remembers: "Tony Hale produced the first two weeks of Jessie's shows from NYC then I went out to produce the next fortnight. I was followed by Declan Meehan (ex-Sunshine and Nova, Dublin). Tony and I stayed in New York City for our stints but Declan got the short straw and had to commute! He would fly out on Thursday, record Sunday's show with Jessie on Friday, produce a live show on Saturday then fly back and hot-foot it to Euston Tower with the tapes in time for the pre-recorded show to go out on Sunday. He did that for several weeks until Jessie's work permit came through and she was able to move back to the UK and join Capital properly."

Chris Cary was then running several stations in Dublin including the very successful *Radio Nova*. He also offered Jessie a job, at a salary she couldn't refuse, although she never really settled down there.

She spent a few months at Radio Luxembourg before heading back stateside, working first on some stations in the Washington DC area and, for a few years, with FSN - the world renowned *Feature Story* international news agency.

Music Director Jessie Brandon at work

A degree in horticulture was next on Jessie's agenda and that remains her passion. In the winter she now works at the Portland Radio Group, a company that has eight radio stations, all in the same building at their Maine headquarters.

Once Jessie had left there was no replacement so the other four DJs (Tommy, Charlie, Holly and David) had to revert to a five-hour shift system. A few days later they were down to just three DJs and adopted a new unofficial strap line "Never be over three days away from the three jock station, Laser 558." This reflected the DJs' frustration with the station never managing more than three days broadcasting before the weather or resupply problems knocked it off the air.

One bit of cheer in December was the announcement that station was now attracting 5 million listeners, according to a market research survey by the MRIB. It showed that 11 percent of the population were tuning in, and that was not counting anyone under 15. 18% of those polled said they were aware of Laser and 9% of UK listeners had tuned in during the previous week. In the south east of England the figures were much higher, 23% in Essex and 14% in London.

The Laser Road Shows were coming in for very close scrutiny by the DTI, who had asked several police forces for assistance in collecting information. In the House of Lords on 12th December, Baroness Stedman asked the Secretary of State why no action had been taken over the Laser Road Show that took place at the St Ivo Centre in St Ives, Cambridgeshire, of which the Radio Regulatory Division had been fully informed.

Baroness Stedman was a director of Hereward Radio, the ILR station with the IBA franchise for Peterborough. Clearly, Hereward Radio were either simply very embarrassed by the success of Laser 558 or the station was seriously damaging their advertising revenues.

Lord Elton replied: "I understand from the Chief Constable of Cambridgeshire that he has sent a report to the Director of Public Prosecutions about the possibility of bringing a prosecution under the Marine Etc. Broadcasting (Offences) Act 1967. I shall write to the noble Baroness when his decision is known."

A week later, in answer to another question, Lord Lucas of Chidworth tolf the House that the DPP is responsible for the prosecution of such offences they are awaiting police reports relating to the Laser Road Shows. These comments and questions in Parliament demonstrate Laser's high profile and how feathers in very high places were being ruffled. Few radio stations ever get mentioned in both of the British houses of Parliament and Laser was getting debates centred around it. It should have been manna from heaven for a PR focussed organisation starved of promotional outlets.

While the DJs technically could not go ashore into the UK, there were times that some did, using the ship's Z-boat which had a powerful motor, or they might hitch a lift on a passing fishing boat, or sightseeing boat run by radio enthusiasts. It was certainly not so easy a trip to make as in the 1960s when ships were only three miles offshore, or off the Dutch coast in the 1970s.

Laser DJs were not quite so 'cut off' as might be thought; they had communications with people on shore via the office in Kent or using a CB, on which many listeners would chat on with the DJs late at night. The Communicator also had a couple of TVs with all four UK channels. There was no direct broadcast satellite TV; Sky TV was only a single channel service.

All the publicity, the success of Laser and an apparent lack of interest by the Government brought in a well known UK music business individual, who claims to have put in £200,000, in cash! A sizeable chunk of this money disappeared; apparently as someone's 'Golden Goodbye' payment.

It is very odd that Lindau blamed the station's economic failure on the people who did the ground work (John Kenning, Paul Hodge, Paul Rusling, Blake Williams, Joe Vogel, etc) when the reason was simply a lack of commercials, which he alone was responsible for selling and which he had promised. He had made same unfulfilled promises for Radio Caroline a few years earlier: "I will bring in at least £10 million a year, from my contacts in the soft drinks and beverages market," Lindau had said.

Dave Chaney at the main 'on air' mixer desk, or control console on the Communicator.

To his left are two triple stack cart' machines on which most music and other items are played out. The Gates console with rotary pots replaced the more 'high-tech' looking mixer by Audio Technics, that Roy Lindau had specified for Laser, purely for cosmetic reasons.

The winter months saw increasingly longer breaks in transmission as fuel runs became fewer and farther between. The last news bulletin went out on Laser just after the New Year when t was it was decided it was taking too long for the depleted crew to assemble the broadcasts.

Another lengthy period of down time occurred again in early January when the aerial became tangled in the masts and needed a partial rebuild. At this time it was too rough to have anyone climb the masts to re-rig the antenna and so the station had to remain off the air until the sea calmed for a few hours.

The repairs lasted only a couple of days before it all came crashing down again and needed yet more repairs, putting the station off the air again. The following day a blizzard bent the top half of one of the ship's fore mast right over. The walls of the mast just buckled through almost 180°. This time a temporary antenna had to be thrown up but would only work at very low power. Reception after dark was almost impossible, even on the Kent coast, just fifteen miles away.

Back in the UK Parliament, their Lordships were again debating unlicensed radio stations. Many members who had invested in ILR franchises complained that their costs were far too high, while unlicensed stations got away with not paying any of the high costs that IBA licenses mandated. While many of the complaints were about the mushrooming 'pirate' scene in London, where there were around two dozen unlicensed stations operating with apparent immunity from prosecution, Baroness Stedman again attacked Laser and Caroline.

"Recently there was an appearance of a *Laser Lover and Communicator Road Show* at the St. Ivo Centre in Huntingdonshire which is a centre owned by the local authority. The managing director of Hereward Radio consulted with the IBA and with the AIRC and they advised that this appearance was in contravention of the Marine Etc. Broadcasting (Offences) Act. The event itself had been plugged on Laser Radio and the roadshow was obviously promoting the interests of this offshore pirate."

"Our MD of Hereward Radio wrote to the Department of Trade and Industry, to the Chief Constable of Cambridgeshire, to the local Member of Parliament, to the district administrator and to the centre management, but the booking went ahead," said the Baroness. "The IBA have written to the Department of Trade and Industry using this as a further example of how little action is being taken against the offshore pirate station, but still to no avail. In this case the police simply sent two officers to observe." That road show was a sell out with two of Laser's star DJs appearing and a party of five DTI staff in attendance, all of whom paid the admission fee, thus helping the enterprise further.

"The IBA have made strong representation to the Government and direct approaches to the Home Secretary, as have the AIRC, but nothing ever happens," continued Baroness Stedman. "If the offshore pirates increase their reach and listeners, then independent local radio is bound to suffer in terms of reach and listeners. Their advertising revenue will diminish and the quality of service, especially the local service to the community, will worsen. If this is allowed to go unchecked and if others take up offshore positions we could end up with all the independent radio stations playing pop music 24 hours a day."

"When will the DTI show that it means business by taking action under its new powers"" she challenged. "When will the Regulatory Investigation Services act decisively and show determination to restore the rule of law in broadcasting matters? When will the Marine Etc. Broadcasting (Offences) Act be enforced against the offshore pirates? These are the questions to which all the ILR stations will want to know the answers, preferably tonight."

The media meanwhile was having a field day speculating about Laser's absence from the airwaves and several newspapers reported that the station was up for sale as a result of the New York's inability to attract any real advertising. Those who were discussing purchasing the station in January 1985 were said to include Chris Cary, Gary Numan and Richard Branson. None of the discussions progressed to a contractual stage but more newspapers repeated the rumours. Many also carried stories to the effect that the station would close if new funding wasn't found by the end of February. One newspaper even put a price tag of £1.5 million on the radio ship and its contents, which may have put off buyers.

By now the radio station was costing about $3,000 a day to operate, but each time it went off the air for a few days, advertisers who were just about to sign got 'cold feet'. They chose to wait to make sure the station was able to broadcast continuously. Each day the DJs would talk up the prospect of the station returning, but all that happened for months was even more breakdowns. Eventually higher power was achieved for a day, but it had the effect of slowing down music as the generator's regulator was not keeping the speed correct causing the frequency of the AC supply to be reduced.

The company's Public Relations executive Jane Morris spoke to several newspapers in London during early February, but succeeded only in alienating some by feeding them erroneous information about the ship. Some had been out to the ship's anchorage and seen the damaged aerial. They saw that no work was being done on the ship and dismissed Laser's official press release stories as mere Public Relations puffery, which indeed they were.

In February some small commercials were at last heard, including *Dickie Dirts*, a chain of clothing retailers in the London area. The Daily Mirror newspaper revealed some news of a planned second radio station, playing easy listening music that was being planned from the Communicator. It's declared intention was to compete with BBC Radio 2, but this story was dismissed by most. People could see that the organisation was struggling to get even one station on the air with any reliability.

Jessie Brandon's long awaited replacement arrived in February in the form of **Chris Carson.** She was a major catch for the station as she speaks English, Dutch and French and was a big fan of the latest music, including Duran Duran, Prince and Frankie Goes to Hollywood. Chris had four years of radio expertise under her belt, most recently at KKRQ in Iowa. She became known on board the ship as "C.C. Rider" which also happened to be one of her favourite Elvis tracks.

Just a week later the Communicator was in trouble once again with yet another dismasting and this time the loss of an anchor too, both on the same night and in a Force 9 gale. After several hours being tossed about in the winter storm they managed to lower a reserve ships anchor. Laser spent the next four days off the air, rebuilding the ship's foremast once again.

On her return to the airwaves, Laser 558 was once again only on the low power setting, so reception was really only possible during the daytime, even close by the ship. Many began to cruelly referring to the station as *Radio Margate*, about the only town where the station could be reliably heard.

Laser's new president, John Moss, put a brave face on the situation and claimed that the station's advertising office in New York was receiving ten enquires a week to buy air time on the station. He claimed that they spend a lot of time turning prospective advertisers away and urging them to use their local station. He also claimed that the station had offered to pay copyright fees to the record companies for the music it played. "The performers are delighted with Laser as we're making their music popular, so its nonsense to say that they are not happy with us playing their records," claimed Mr Moss.

In an article in The Guardian newspaper, John Moss also had plenty to say about the alleged interference with the Irish RTE station. "One time when there was an important Gaelic football commentary on. We closed down for the duration of the game, but still got complaints of interference so it can't have been us!"

Moss also said that 70% of the demonstration tapes that the station received from prospective employees for DJ jobs on the ship were from women. Initially the station had only one female DJ on the air, Jessie Brandon, but in future there would be an even mixture of four female and four male DJs on the ship, serving two-month stints with one month off.

While the station was off air another two new female DJs were brought on board to replace Rick Harris who was going on holiday. They were Liz West and Erin Kelly. The first programme that Erin did she held tightly on to a bucket in the studio for over an hour, she was so seasick. Erin came from New Orleans, Alabama and had been in radio for nine years, most recently at WVNA in Muscle Shoals, Alabama. She also worked as a professional photographer for a while and she was a green belt in karate.

The following day Tommy Rivers took over breakfast duties and the latest new girl took to the air late in the evening, **Liz West.** A real radio professional, "Dizzy Miss Lizzy", as she was called on board the Communicator, hailed from Florida but joined Laser straight from a radio gig in Palm Springs, California. She had previously worked at WDIZ in Orlando (thus her nickname) and at 98 Rock in Tampa. Liz was a total radio professional and was appointed Music Director.

In an interview with the Offshore Echos magazine, Liz said she originally joined Laser as a challenge, because she had always wanted to tour Europe. Laser offered its DJs thirteen weeks holiday a year, which was of great appeal to Liz's self-confessed wanderlust.

Liz told Offshore Echos that she thought that Laser was successful because most other stations are too varied and not formatted correctly. "We are Americans, so there is a dash of novelty there, and we play all the hits. We play proven, charted hits all day."

Not the holiday Liz West expected

Laser's trio of girls attracted a lot more positive press coverage for Laser 558 in February 1985, which took some attention from the station's woes over its antenna problems and financial difficulties. The new President of the station, John Moss, was quoted in many publications saying, "Liz, Chris and Erin offer a vitality and energy that our audience will delight in. Their voices and presentation are of an extremely high calibre and we are proud that they have chosen Laser as a platform for their talent. Our listeners are going to love them."

Moss claimed that the station had taken about a quarter of a million dollars over the previous six months but needed to hit $100,000 a month to be profitable. They had extraordinary high expenses due to operating three or four bases and had to maintain a presence and staff in six or seven countries, which had been a logistical nightmare and not at all cheap.

On many occasions, the authorities have used an old chestnut that, unless properly maintained, powerful broadcast transmitters on ships could cause interference to other communications. Offshore radio stations invariably use professional equipment, which is always fitted with harmonic suppressors, to avoid any emissions on other than their correct frequency.

Radio signals going out over other frequencies means less energy on the desired frequency, so its not something that any radio station wants, much less do they want to cause any problems to communications, or 'safety of life' radio transmissions. Laser's equipment was a pair of new transmitters from a reputable company, *CSI Transmitters* of Boca Raton in Florida. They met every possible requirement for the suppression of spurious RF and harmonics, as indeed did the slightly older equipment on the MV Ross Revenge used by Radio Caroline. Both stations used very similar equipment to that used by the BBC and major broadcasters everywhere.

On 20th February, the British Government's coastal radio station at North Foreland contacted the ships, as it was experiencing interference with its main distress frequency, 500 kHz. This is close to Laser's 558 kHz frequency, so Laser offered to close down as a test, however the interference continued.

Radio Caroline, who were then on 576 kHz, also closed momentarily, yet still the interference on 500kHz continued. Eventually it was found that the problem was the BBC's half a million watt transmissions on 648 kHz, from Orfordness, were mixing with BBC Radio 1 and causing an inter-modulation product.

The coast station immediately apologised and wished the Laser crew Good Luck. There was regular contact with the coast guards and other officials, although the coast station was prohibited from connecting the ships to the public phone system for calls. They always handle urgent calls when required, and in return the radio ships monitored their own area for weather abnormalities etc, unofficially, for the authorities. The following day Dave Lee Stone departed the ship for a holiday and Laser 558 was back on five-hour shows due to the small number of DJs, with three quarters of the station's daily output now being presented by female DJs. The girls collectively adopted the name 'Laserettes".

The last week of February was problematic as the station could only broadcast for a few hours a day on very low power. Work continue out on deck for about a week, replacing and strengthening the foremast but it was very difficult time as, with the bitter cold out at sea, the riggers could only work for short periods. At one stage they were about to go back on the air when a sudden squall came out of nowhere.

The aerial cables hanging loosely from the masts were literally torn from their mountings and the crew could only watch helplessly as their hard work was undone. After several more days hard work they got the mast back up, and in fact it was now ten feet higher than before, which it was hoped would enable a stronger signal to be radiated.

Charlie Wolf appeared on Channel Four TV's 'The Tube' show in early March and thanked Laser's listeners in the UK for their support during the station's winter of discontent. He got over two minutes of prime time on screen publicity and told how the music was all delivered to the ship via the satellite link from its New York office.

Despite the Seawolf's protests that the station was legal, presenter Jools Holland explained to viewers that the station was illegal and it was illegal to listen to it. This would probably have given Laser considerable cachet among the stations young and somewhat rebellious audience.

Some advertising was now being heard, whenever the station was on the air, including spots for Virgin Airlines, Terrapin Computer Games and KonTiki Holidays. The latest radio listening figures for the Netherlands showed that 8% of Dutch listeners were now tuning to offshore stations, almost two thirds of them to Radio Caroline. New station, Radio Monique, named after the ex wife of Fred Bolland, which also broadcast from the Caroline ship, Ross Revenge, was getting about 2% of the Dutch listeners and Laser just over 1%.

Returning to the Communicator in March, DJ Charlie Wolf poked fun at the crew of the Suffolk police boat, the Ian Jacob of Ipswich, who had visited the ships that day to take pictures. He thanked them for delivering newspapers and beer but asked them to bring milk next time, as he is teetotal. The same day, Michael Dean made one of his rare appearances on the air; he was a ship's steward whose real job was to take care of the crew's welfare on the ship but had often guested in the DJ's shows with culinary tips and lots of health quips.

The authorities were by now regularly appearing alongside the radio ships and occasionally stopped supply boats, questioning those on board. They were empowered to do so as most of the visitors were British vessels sailing out from UK ports. Foreign registered vessels could not be stopped while in international waters, except by warships of their own country, although they could be stopped if they came into British territorial waters of course.

By the middle of March, the numbers of staff were so short and some of those who were on board so affected by the weather, that engineer Joe Vogel was pressed into service as a DJ again. He wore his 'Mighty Joe Young' hat to present shows, while Michael Dean also had to leave his normal spot in the Communicator's galley to operate the studio and host programmes.

In the middle of March some new components were personally delivered to the ship by Laser's new president, John Moss. This enabled the station to run one transmitter on near full power of 22 kilowatts, the first time the Communicator had been able to make this power level since it moved from 729 to 558 kHz.

A press release from MMI, the New York advertising agency selling the station, announced that Bradley Urghetta had been appointed international account executive. Brad had worked in sales at WRC-FM in Washington, an NBC station.

Laser went even more international later in March, jointly hosting a Laser Road show in Holland with Dutch station Radio Monique. Laser DJ Tommy Rivers appeared at the first of these joint ventures in the Dutch naval port of Den Helder. The event, in the Huys Tijdverdrijf, was full for the event and visitors were also entertained by Nico van der Stee, a DJ from Radio Monique.

At the end of March it was revealed that one of Laser's original DJs, Dave Lee Stone, had been signed by Radio Luxembourg. 25-year-old Dave had a warm laid-back style and was also responsible for Laser's broadcast style and music content. He did his final programme on Laser in April 1985.

Laser had upset several media folk in the UK, mainly by spreading false stories for the past year about its owner and the *modus operandi* of the station. Bitchy comments were now beginning to appear in the trade press, belittling the station as well as reminding prospective advertisers that it was still illegal for British companies to advertise on the station.

Articles in *Campaign, Broadcast* and *Media Week* ran conflicting articles quoting a variety of 'station representatives' called John Charles, John Cole, John Elliott, Paul Fairs and Robbie Day. The station's New York office said that these were all imposters and that Laser had no office at all in London. "I've never met these guys," claimed John Moss, the President of MMI. "They are just a bunch of chancers, trying to get into our knickers!"

A company called *Overseas Media Inc* had two offices in London, both 'rent-a-desk' operations, in Kensington and in Earl's Court. John Catlett oversaw them, although he often used another name. These were widely known as offices of Laser's London operation, along with one in Mortimer Street close to Broadcasting House.

An American calling himself "John Charles" was a regular visitor to record company offices in London where he assured music business folk that he was the General Manager of Laser 558. He was quoted in Media Week as saying; "I don't have a very high visibility and my whereabouts are not bandied about, in order for me to touch base with people in those countries where we may not operate legally."

"If I came into England using my own identity, the Government might not want me here and they could stop me entering," explained Mr Charles. He claimed to have managed a number of radio stations in the US and to have owned a radio station in Connecticut. He told the magazine's reporters that he had spent a fortnight out on the Communicator, but spent a lot of his time searching for new DJs to recruit.

On 12th April during a force nine storm the Communicator was adrift once again and silent after the new antenna took a battering from the storm. The ship's engines performed well and soon brought her back to her regular position.

Erin Kelly revealed to listeners that her colleague Dave Lee Stone had managed to sleep through the whole episode, but that she had managed to film the entire cruise. "It was the craziest ride I ever had, with huge seas crashing into the side of the ship, but thanks to our able-bodied seamen on board we have come through it all. Look out for the movie in your cinemas soon!"

Just a few days later the Communicator was bathed in glorious sunshine and Erin was able to shoot the entire crew of seamen and DJs sunbathing out on Splinter Beach, the first time in 1985 it had been sunny enough to do so. The day was noted in the Communicator's official logbook as the start of *Eurotan 85*, but there were to be lots of chilling moments ahead for the station.

Forbes magazine, an American magazine that focuses on wealth and the wealthy, ran a big article about the Communicator and Laser 558 in its April edition.

It was helpful in that it brought the station to the eyes of those with sufficient funds to keep the stations going, but it never brought in any further investment. This is surprising, especially given that knowledge of the station being at an all time high.

Laser had now been mentioned in both houses of Parliament and in the world's leading magazine for the rich. The Forbes article said:

> *It's an odd story. The Government think they know best and kill any competition, until entrepreneurs figure out a way to give the public what they want and to make money from it. This time the old story is being played out on the North Sea on a former survey ship anchored 14 miles from Britain.*
>
> *There, Charlie Wolf, a disc jockey from Utah and seven American cronies risk the gales to run Laser 558, a new radio station backed by US investors. It plays hit music, advertises US goods and shakes up broadcasters across Europe. They are all having a marvellous time out on the high seas.*

St George's Day 1985 dawned with a severe storm warning in force for the Thames sea area and Michael Dean being pressed into action at the two triple stack cart machines to deputise for Liz West. She later described the weather as the worst she had ever experienced. "It was just horrendous, the Communicator was twisting every which way you can imagine, everything was crashing down in the galley and in the studios. There were cart's flying everywhere, as well as the remnants of someone's lunch spilled across the desk. To walk anywhere was difficult and it was impossible to sit down. I lay in my bunk and just cried for a couple of hours."

The northeasterly gale brought huge waves rolling along the Knock Deep. Waves from the Northeast are always highest as this is the only direction to which there was no protection from the sandbanks.

The Communicator was tossed and turned all day, pitching and tossing on the port reserve anchor and during one pirouette at just before 5pm the front mast buckled over, putting the station off the air once again.

Damage to the front mast in April 1985

During the next two weeks a completely new front mast had to be erected on the ship, using new mast sections, reinforced with additional bracing at the flanges and joints.

An article in the Evening Standard on May Day (while the station was still silent with a badly bent antenna mast) announced that the latest recruit for Laser has royal connections. **Craig Novack** was a distant cousin of the Princess of Wales.

"Diana Spencer and I have the same great, great, great grandfather who was a pork packer from Ohio called John Wood. Our family seat is in Wortley near Sheffield, and the Princess's father, Earl Spencer, is one of my uncles."

Craig boasted a First Class degree in Business Studies, not to mention a wealth of radio experience on radio stations in Detroit and Massachusetts; he now owns small chain of stations in New York. At 6 foot 5 inches tall, Syracuse-born Craig was one of the tallest guys on the ship, which made him very useful at times, although it did give him a sore head too until he learned to remember to duck when going through the ship's 'restricted height' doorways.

Craig had plenty of time to get used to the ship and the sea, as he was unable to go on the air straight away. When he arrived at the ship it was just after a huge storm that had brought down the front mast. He found all the DJ crew were out on deck pitching in to lend a hand building the new antenna mast. Even the Laserettes, Liz West and Chris Carson, were out on deck braving the cold conditions. And without a moment's thought to personal cost!

"The thing is dear listeners, Liz has sacrificed three of her legendary fingernails for this venture and we should just take a second right now in memory for those three nails that she gave so lovingly for the cause," quipped Chris Carson on the air.

"That's right," replied Liz, who was co-hosting the first show heard on the air after the rebuilding of the mast, on the 7th May. "I have lost three of them! And there is so much dirt and stuff under the remaining seven fingernails, which has never happened in my entire life," she exclaimed, sounding mortified at the thought. Asked if they should now have a minute's silence for the fingernails Liz showed that she still had a tiny bit of her wicked sense of humour left when she said "I think we've had quite enough silence over these last few weeks on the 558 frequency!"

A few days later the London Evening Standard ran another large piece about Laser, remarking on the growing links between the station and Richard Branson's Virgin empire. DJs on the station were enthusiastically promoting the Virgin Atlantic on which they had free First Class air tickets for their trips between London and the USA. As the deal was arranged by both Virgin and Laser's offices in New York they were not breaking the Marine Offences Act. Richard Branson said that he was "not personally involved in every aspect of the airline's operation but was pleased that Laser was kind to Virgin on the air."

Virgin were not the only organisation cooperating with the ship as the Time Out listings magazine were also swapping favours and gave Laser a lot of publicity. "We are totally sympathetic with the liberation of the airwaves and are 100 per cent behind Laser," said Tony Elliott, one of the magazine's publishers. "Laser's 5 million listeners prove that it is what people have wanted for ages."

May was the first time that Laser openly admitted that it was accepting payola for playing records on the air with some regular plays being heralded as Laser Spot Songs. The station had long been overtly running short (30 or 60 seconds) commercials for new releases and now these were formally played in their entirety and bill boarded as Laser Spot Songs at the start and the finish.

Some of the American DJs had been uncomfortable about plug records being played, as this was not openly done in American radio. There had been big problems with payola many years earlier when some DJs were accepting gifts from pluggers (in the form of cash, drugs, holidays and even female favours for the DJs). These had been collected by DJs personally, without them going through the radio stations' books. The practice had however long been an established practice in Europe. Radio Luxembourg and Radio Caroline had long benefitted from such payments and in the early 1970s some BBC producers were fired for the practice of payola. It is not however an offence for a radio station to accept 'pay for play, just the DJ to have his own deals.

The station was once again broadcasting at full power just in time to promote Laser's first birthday celebrations. A big party was organised in London for the big day on the 24th May and was extensively promoted on the air. It was to be at the London Hippodrome, the most high profile venue at that time in the West End. Suddenly, the day before the event the on air plugs stopped and the 'event cancelled' notice went up at the door.

"The police came on to us very strongly and in a tough manner said we must cancel or they could prosecute," explained the club owner, Peter Stringfellow. "I was happy to accept the booking at first because I didn't think there was anything wrong. It wasn't something I was taking a stance over, it was simply a commercial booking.'

The police action was requested by the DTI (the Department of Trade & Industry) who monitor radio stations in the UK. When they heard about the party during their monitoring of the station, they informed the Director of Public Prosecutions that it could be in breach of the law on the grounds that it was publicising an unlicensed station.

Laser 558 had to celebrate its first birthday on 24th May alone as the weather out in the Thames Estuary was far too rough for visitors. A small plane flew over London with a banner wishing the station well and many special programme items were aired, including the station's entire jingle package and a repeat of the station's opening at 5am a year earlier, which almost everyone had missed the first time around.

Some Laser souvenirs are still available
including historical recordings, jingles and T-shirts, etc:
(See *http://worldofradio.co.uk/Laser.html*)

The next day, Laser's recently promoted General Manager John Catlett wrote an article in the Times newspaper, explaining how radio pirates could rescue radio in the UK. He explained:

"Laser Radio is called a pirate, and while this is a picturesque, picaresque description, it is wrong. Laser may be buccaneering, operating as it does from a ship in international waters, but it breaks no laws."

"In Britain it is accused of stealing its frequency because that is one of dozens of frequencies allocated to, but not used by the BBC. Laser selected the frequency with care to avoid interference with existing stations and communications essential to marine safety, following the tradition of Radio Luxembourg and Vatican Radio, both of which broadcast long before they needed the sanction of any international body."

"As it celebrates its first birthday, the station has gained five million listeners a week in Britain, where commercial radio is in a mess. With a few notable exceptions commercial radio fails to deliver what advertisers and listeners want. It tries to be all things to all people: local and national, music and information oriented, and aimed at young and old people."

"In trying to serve so many masters, commercial radio in Britain serves no one well. Different people want different things from their radio. The costs of producing radio programmes are so low, and so many frequencies are available that there is no good reason to deprive the public of as many different programmes that creative minds can devise."

"Why is it that New York, a city smaller than London, can support more than 70 radio stations when in London the authorities permit only 7 to be heard? This is not a matter of physics, but one of politics and vested interests. Laser Radio is programmed in the belief that a certain section of European population want to hear hit music uninterrupted by talk. Many people have no desire to listen to station such as Laser and their tastes should be met elsewhere. But many millions DO want such a station. Who after all owns the frequencies? Is it the Government's broadcasting organisations or the people themselves?"

"The most vocal critic of Laser in Britain is the commercial radio stations. Are they really, as they claim, trying to protect the excellence of British commercial radio or are they simply trying to protect their monopoly?"

"Commercial radio in Britain attracts little more than two percent of all advertising expenditure. In America, where the figure is nearer eight per cent, the radio industry is vibrant and strong. Commercial radio there succeeds by providing what people want."

"Rather than fighting Laser's existence, British radio stations should welcome the competition and work with us to improve standards on commercial radio. Then perhaps Britain's radio as well as its television will become the envy of the world."

Those thought provoking words shook many cabinet ministers as well as those who were in charge of the UK's commercial radio stations, and the IBA who licensed the country's commercial radio stations. When Home Secretary William Whitelaw spoke to Prime Minister Margaret Thatcher about it a few days later she was already aware of the piece and asked that urgent thought be given to making urgent changes to the commercial radio industry.

John Catlett's article also had a tremendous effect within in the IBA, which within weeks was consulting on such contentious matters as allowing stations to split their AM and FM transmissions to offer alternative services. They also began planning a new tier of community radio, and looked again at expanding stations small and large, adding regional radio to its remit.

Advertising executives agreed that the only way to expand the advertising cake might be to allow some stations to broadcast a national station as that was clearly what the largest advertisers wanted. The TV lobby however prevented this happening for some years but eventually new legislation was enacted that permitted the creation of three new national commercial radio stations. The authorities however were widely perceived as one of the biggest barriers to the development of radio and so the all powerful IBA was to be cut down to size, replaced by a new *Radio Authority* and a similar body for television.

10. LASER 558 – THE FINAL SUMMER

With five million listeners in the UK, almost as many on the continent and financial support finally trickling through, the summer looked like being a good one for Laser 558. It was also, however, to be its last. Little further work was done during the summer on the flimsy antenna system neither on the station's infrastructure. Laser finally however had a General Manager in John Catlett who knew and loved radio, as well as a popular team of DJs.

Many of the adverts being heard were placed by small companies unable to pay the huge airtime fees which Laser's rate card requested and many of them were "cash in a carrier bag" arrangements. One of the biggest problems for the organisation since before the launch was that the New York sales office cost far more to run than the radio station itself. One of John Catlett's first acts once he took the reins was to close the swanky suite contracted by Roy Lindau in mid-Manhattan. He opened a smaller facility further up at 515 Madison, which was only a fraction the cost but still as functional. "We were spending more money on the New York sales office than we were on the Communicator and the entire crew; it just made no sense to have that kind of expenditure," he explained.

The move coincided with a change to the station's address. DJs stopped announcing Madison Avenue as the street address and used a PO Box facility at the Grand Central Station for listener mail. In a Readers' Poll, a British music weekly newspaper, the Melody Maker showed the entire team of Laser 558 DJs being voted in 5th place, behind the established BBC DJs John Peel, Steve Wright, Janice Long and Anne Nightingale, who all had prime slots on BBC Radio 1.

Instead of the much vaunted pan-European and global advertising that Lindau had spent a fortune chasing, most of the commercial income for Laser 558 was now coming from small more entrepreneurial companies in the London area. Those advertisers were acutely aware of the impact of the station and so were a much easier sell, even though such spots were illegal. They included films, books, music, holidays and other high margin goods and services which relied on high profile marketing, for which Laser 558 was ideal!

Some of the advertising deals were often struck by a small group of salesmen with little or no idea of business and a lot of the money raised never found its way to the radio station. Much less found its way to the radio ship, where supplies and conditions dwindled down to pitiful levels, a situation that was about to worsen.

Less than a month after the first birthday celebrations, some big changes to the station's 'on air' sound took place.

Laser's first DJ, Rick Harris

The disc jockey who opened the radio station, Rick Harris, presented his breakfast show for the final time. He never mentioned on the air that is was to be his final programme on Laser, but simply never came back.

Rick had felt for some time that the station had now suffered too many breakdowns and lost too much airtime. He was keen to make a success of his career and had another job waiting.

That very same night a recorded announcement replaced Charlie Wolf's show. The unidentified voice announced that "Contractual negotiations between Mr Wolf and Laser 558's operating company, Eurad SA, had reached a critical point". Laser 558 closed down early that night as the remaining crew spent the night engaged in a flurry of calls and discussions.

The following day, Laser 558 programming continued without reference to the previous day's disruption, with Charlie back in his regular nighttime slot. Rick meanwhile moved to Dublin where he was soon heard for a few months on Radio Nova, by now broadcasting from the Nova country club at Rathfarnham. He then went back to the States and joined WGMX in Norwalk, Ct before going back to university to do a degree in IT.

As well as the big changes on the air, there was more disruption ashore, with the station's Public Relations representative, Jane Morris telling anyone who would listen that she had left Laser. Morris claimed that she not been paid for her efforts on the station's behalf and was not prepared to work for Laser for nothing. It was a story that had been heard many times before from Laser employees.

The station had run some 'Marlborough Country' programmes that were ostensibly sponsored by Marlborough cigarettes, however there had been disputes as to the payment route of the fees, or whether the station should carry cigarette commercials. The deal had been quietly dropped, although the programmes still were heard from time to time, as no one ever told the DJs on the Communicator!

At the end of June listeners were suddenly treated to a new show – "**Scott Shannon**'s American Top 30. The programme was scheduled up against the long-standing Top 20 slot on Radio Luxembourg, which had been running a weekly Top 20 chart countdown at that time since the late 1950s.

Top New York DJ Scott Shannon joined Laser

Scott who had invented the 'Morning Zoo' concept in Tampa Florida in the early eights and brought it to WHTZ in New York when it launched in summer 1983. *Scott Shannon's American Top 40* was produced by Westwood One in Los Angeles. The giant syndication company were paying $400 a week for the slot, from which they could have sold the airtime for over $2,000 at rate card prices. Whoever paid whom and however much, the DJs on board the Communicator didn't benefit from any of it, other than getting some time off while the programmes ran.

Westwood One was a comparatively new radio syndication company formed by Norman Pattitz, a TV advertising executive in Los Angeles. He was in the middle of trying to buy out *Mutual Broadcasting*, one of the 'big four' American networks in 1985 and thought that having some of his product aired on stations in Europe with wide coverage might add a sweetener to the deal.

At the end of the following week a long article in the weekly Broadcast magazine told of poor morale on the ship. "Laser 558 has been suffering cash flow problems and its DJs are having to wait from 4 to 6 weeks to get paid. The shortage of funds was exacerbated by a lengthy closedown the previous month while its antenna system was replaced as all their funds had to be diverted to make repairs, "I've personally gone for several weeks without being paid," claimed MMI's president, John Moss.

Another syndicated programme started each Saturday night in the first week of July. **Mary Turner** was a well-known interviewer of top music business artists; her "Off The Record" show was slotted into prime time.

Mary conducted an interview with the rock band Queen in 1984, which became so much of a sought after collectors item among Queen fans that the discs were soon selling for over $1,000 each. It was reported in the music press that May's programmes featuring the Kinks and the Dublin band U2 heard on Laser had been paid for by the artists concerned.

As Laser had few adverts scheduled, especially at night, some of the programmes would under run, i.e. end before their allotted time. All that could be heard on Laser on those occasions was several minutes of dead air, until someone realised the pre-recorded show had ended and went to the studio to play something else!

Mary Turner

The show had been offered to Laser free of charge as a programme 'fill' to help promote the Westwood One name, as the syndicator was for sale. They were an optional extra, for Laser's own sales team to sell advertising for it

Other syndicated programmes appeared from time to time; **Dr Demento** is well known in the USA for his peculiar brand of humour. His shows had carried on some stations and now they were to be tried out on the British public in an experiment, but in the early hours of the morning, and just once a month.

Dr Demento's shows were very much 'a cult thing' and contained mainly parodies of well-known hits. Some of the tracks played were his own recordings, under the of Weird Al Jankowitz. The humour was probably 'over the heads' of most listeners in Europe; at that time in the early hours of the morning it probably sounded quite incomprehensible to most listeners. Demento was well over forty in 1984, making him Laser's oldest DJ, but he's still broadcasting today.

Laser 558 signed yet another female DJ in July. In the mid eighties, ladies were still quite a rarity on British radio stations. **Jonell Pernula** was the latest signing, who promptly dropped her Finnish surname, believing it too difficult for listeners in some countries to understand. Laser by now had listeners in seven other countries as well as the UK.

By the end of the month Jonell had been promoted to the station's breakfast programme where she usually sounded very fresh and enthusiastic, except when she overslept! Jonell had originally been working on a country music station called KTOE in Minneapolis. Her engagement as a DJ on Laser was the work of Tommy Rivers, who was also from Minnesota. Jonell joined the station on a short-term deal for just a couple of months, to help out with staff shortages while other DJs took their holidays.

Following the worldwide success of the Live Aid event in July 1985, Charlie Wolf decided to try and launch his own charity to help out the BBC which was being subjected to some high profile cuts to its budget. It was called BEEB AID.

Charlie had heard the news that, over at the BBC, everything must be cut by a half. He feared that meant Radio 4 would be cut in half also, so it would become Radio 2! The idea of BEEB AID was enthusiastically taken up by Laser's colleagues on nearby Radio Caroline. They had often helped the BBC out; some years ago they relayed a BBC daily soap called *Mrs Dale's Diary*, as there were rumours that its audiences were dwindling. Radio Caroline this time offered to donate some of their home brewed beer to help Charlie Wolf's idea of a charity record to help fund their BEEB AID charity.

Another new female crew member appeared on the Communicator in August. **Fiona Jeffreys**, was hired to cook for the crew since Michael Dean had now left the ship. Fiona was persuaded to join the Communicator from Radio Caroline where she was already a very popular DJ having joined the station over the previous winter. Fiona's sultry and suggestive tones were ideal for male listeners to get them through a cold night! Fiona now has three grown up children and recently gave up her career as a teacher. She now concentrates on the family's business, near their home in the East Midlands.

'Eurosiege 85'

During the second week in August a UK Government Minster, Geoffrey Pattie, announced that the DTI would be chartering a vessel to carry out an observation exercise to see who was supplying the ships. If the supplies were coming from the UK or involved British subjects, they would be stopped and reported for committing offences under the Marine Offences Act.

The DTI chartered a 99-foot long seagoing launch from Trinity House called the 'Dioptric Surveyor' that would be stationed between the two radio ships in the Knock Deep. The announcements were covered in most of the UK's print and TV media and as soon as the vessel turned up on the 8th of August, Laser immediately gave the DTI's initiative a lot of 'on air' publicity.

Cheerleading Laser's ridicule of the DTI being their new neighbour was DJ Charlie Wolf, who had spent the previous week telling listeners that he was about to leave, having become a bit demoralised with life on the Communicator. Now the DTI had put some spice in his life and were instrumental in his staying!

The exercise to watch the radio ships had little effect initially as it was strictly a 9 to 5 operation; the DTI only showed up 'on station' from about 10 am to 4pm each day. By only making deliveries to the ships after dark, suppliers for both radio ships could operate with impunity.

SPY BOAT: The Dioptric Surveyor, chartered by the DTI

The DTI's tiny boat was not very stable in the open sea. It was fine for ferrying experienced sea pilots and other seamen about, but the DTI bureaucrats who had no sea legs described the trips on it as "a total nightmare." Most were terribly seasick and several staff refused to serve on it.

The 'daytime only' situation didn't last long because the Dioptric Surveyor was fitted with large searchlights and night vision goggles. They also had the back up of being able to call out a helicopter to help them spot supplies being delivered under the cover of darkness. The DTI confirmed that they were serious about the operation; they issued a Press Release saying that the launch had been chartered indefinitely and was costing around £50,000 a month to operate.

"They are trying to starve us out," said Laser spokesman John Catlett. "This is being done at enormous expense to the British tax payers but we shall never give in. We tender our ship from Spain, and we are not doing anything illegal."

Catlett told reporters that it was typical of the British Government to presume that records and food could not be obtained from anywhere else but the UK. "We're prepared to continue broadcasting and being American we do not break any laws. It seems to me that if the British Government want to spend £50,000 a month to watch who supplies us, they are welcome to, but I expect the British listeners will not be happy at paying the bill for that."

The DJs on the two radio ships saw their new neighbour (the DTI boat) as a spy ship and it was usually referred to on Laser 558 as such. The Laser DJs adopted a single, called "Laser Love" by the band 'After the Fire' as a new station theme tune from the middle of August. It had been a minor hit in the UK five years previously.

The antics out in the Thames estuary were a bonus for some newspapers and they revelled in the 'David and Goliath' battle taking place on the airwaves. Neil Wallis from the Daily Star stocked up a fishing boat called the Freeward with supplies and copies of his newspaper and made a run out to the Laser ship. The following day he wrote in The Star how he and the other visitors had been well received at Radio Caroline and at Laser 558, but that the po-faced Westminster Wallies were not even out there to welcome them!

"The 'Men from the Ministry' apparently spend the nights and the rough weather days tied up in Harwich harbour," the Star explained to their readers. "Petticoat Pirate DJ Liz West whooped for joy to get a Star T-Shirt and a copy of the newspaper, telling us it was the first she had seen in months."

Neil's supply boat hang around for a couple of hours, toasting the absent spy ship with champagne but the DTI didn't show up for the party. The Daily Star had proved that not only were the DTI wasting public money, but they weren't even doing their job well.

Laser 558 began playing a new version of the 1960s disco hit *I Spy for the FBI*. It had been re-recorded by some members of the bands 'Sad Café' and 'Boys Don't Cry' as well as Paul Young. Laserettes Liz West and Erin Kelly could also be heard on it. An energetic up-tempo song it poked fun at the Whitehall servants charged with monitoring the station, but it was not released until mid October.

The Sunday Times pointed out in an article that the DTI was now helping Laser get written about in lots of publications previously wary of mentioning the station. John Catlett, GM of Laser confirmed the story: "We are getting calls from a lot of potential advertisers who hadn't previously considered us. A lot of new advertisers are now wanting to buy time on our station, but for now we are determined to stay within the law and stay on as legal a basis as possible."

The Three Laserettes had by now become very popular with listeners, just as Jessie Brandon had before them. While Charlie Wolf was the most controversial and without doubt a highlight on the station, it was the girls who were getting noticed. They were in high demand for newspaper and other interviews and they pulled lots of mail from avid listeners. Had Laser 558 been selling photographs of the Laserettes they could probably have made a fortune!

The Laserettes did give the station a unique sound, not only because they had American accents, but because they were at times on the air for long shifts of up to five hours. One female DJ was unusual in Europe, but to have three on the air consecutively made Laser stand out more and almost gave it cult status.

Laserettes Chris Carson, Liz West and Erin Kelly
by Chris Edwards, OEM

One visitor to the Communicator during Euroseige was former Laser 558 DJ David Chaney. He was now working at KMET in Los Angeles but while on the ship he produced a commercial for a record album that could be ordered by mail order from an address in The Hague, but the product was never shipped .

Also available by mail order was a T-Shirt produced by the Laser Road Show, with the slogan 'I Spy for the DTI'. Advertising was now being booked in increasing quantities, but most orders were from small mail order operators. Video recorders, champagne, pop concerts and records were all heard.

On 21st August, the thirteenth day of Eurosiege 85, the MV Communicator upped anchor from her position of one and a half miles south of the Ross Revenge, and sailed north about ten miles to a position. Here she was about half a mile from the main shipping lane into Harwich, and she was followed all the way by the DTI boat, the Dioptric Surveyor. With a force eight storm forecast the Communicator returned to her old anchorage two days later.

DJ Charlie Wolf later explained why the Communicator had made the little cruise to the north of the regular anchorage. "We wanted to see what the DTI would do when we moved. As we suspected, they were really watching us and not very interested in Radio Caroline. We were exposed to the open sea out there and the Caroline ship was sheltered in the Knock Deep, so could possibly have been tendered at that time, but they just left her unwatched to keep an eye on us. So it confirmed what we needed to know: as the big mouthed, noisy and 'in your face' Americans we were the real target of Euroseige!" This is something that would be confirmed again quite firmly, but not for a couple of months yet.

By now almost 20 TV crews had been out to the Communicator to film pieces for TV news programmes, probably the most publicity that any radio station has ever achieved in such a short period of time. By the end of August, Erin Kelly had slipped ashore for the last time, choosing not to return to the ship. She was very unhappy at the standard of food on board the Communicator and the lack of fresh water for washing.

During this time, regular updates were being given to listeners on the spy ship, often in a very light hearted manner with much merriment and humour at the expense of the DTI observers on the Dioptric Surveyor. These were usually during Charlie Wolf's programme each evening when he made "Live reports from my vantage point on the poop deck of the Communicator".

A particularly brilliant 'wind up' was a spoof commercial that Laser ran for "Anoraks DTI', parodying the well known listeners organisation, *Anoraks UK*. The commercials suggested that, as DTI were photographing the ships anyway, they were now selling copies of their photographs to radio fans. The spoof adverts suggested that the DTI needed to raise some money to help pay for the spy boat. As well as 'spy boat', the Dioptric Surveyor had also been given a new name and was often referred to as the Moronic Surveyor.

Charlie Wolf further teased the DTI spies, as well as Laser bosses, by claiming that he was about to join an ILR station when he next went on holiday. After building up the big announcements over a couple of days he confided to Laser 558 listeners that it would be *Chipping Sodbury Sound*, a fictitious parody.

In August Liz West left the Communicator after a ten week stay on board and did not return. She was left penniless at an hotel in Kent. Out of funds and getting no support from the station, supporters of the station organised a collection for her to get a ticket back to the USA and she left a few weeks later. Liz later appeared on Radio Luxembourg as the station's first ever female DJ, but didn't stay very long before heading back to a job in Virginia. Liz died in 2002 aged only 40.

On the 30th August the Dioptric Surveyor spy ship was suddenly replaced by a larger boat called the Farne for two days, as she needed urgent repairs. A week later the spy boat disappeared again and at first she seemed to have been replaced by a Dutch Minesweeper, the 'Makkum'. Charlie Wolf's Mickey-taking was a bit more subdued as he wasn't sure if the warship carried any armaments. During their exercises they did eventually make contact with Laser and confirmed that they were not in the Knock Deep to watch the radio ships at all, not even the Dutch station (Radio Monique) on board the Ross Revenge.

The spy boat's next replacement was due to the threat from severe weather approaching. A robust little Harwich tug called the Grey Echo took over and then a week later HM Customs boat called the Safeguard took up position.

Plans were mooted in September to strengthen the aerial masts on the Communicator, and use both transmitters together so that perhaps 40 kilowatts power output might be possible. The organisation however had left things a bit too close to winter and the tales were later revealed as a story simply put out to encourage the DJs on board to stay. It was impossible to get new equipment and riggers to the ship now with the DTI watching over their shoulder most of the time. It was proving almost impossible to get regular supplies.

The DTI began putting up public notices at all the ports around Kent and Essex in the middle of September warning boat owners that if they ferried people or stories out to radio ships they could be prosecuted. A similar exercise had been undertaken in the 1970s when the Government had rather belatedly heard that supply runs from the UK might have been taking place.

This exercise was pretty futile as the boats being used to ferry supplies to both radio ships were regulars. Neither of the radio ships were going out shopping for a supply boat to use, so the 'ad hoc' business that the DTI were seeking to prevent simply didn't exist! Indeed, while Radio Caroline used several boatmen in France, Belgium, Essex and Kent, Laser used only one supply company, whose MD had become the project's local Operations Manager, so lucrative was the business.

The DTI officials proved inefficient in their observation and often seemed to be outrun by crews of both ships. The presence of the spy boat was only a minor irritation to Radio Caroline, which was able to come through the DTI's Euroseige campaign unscathed. Laser however were to be badly affected by the 'blockade and had great difficulty in getting supplies to the ship at times. With a bit wiser investment and more experienced management they could have overcome the problems they faced.

A few days later Essex pop star Gary Numan flew his plane out over the radio ships and dipped his wings to salute the MV Communicator. He was a keen radio enthusiast who was very grateful for the exposure that Laser 558 and Radio Caroline had given his recent singles, including 'Change your Mind' which the BBC had ignored. Numan had just launched his own record label in 1984 and Laser had put his releases on 'hot' rotation.

DJ Jonell in the main 'on air' studio

The DTI's blockade was being felt most on the Communicator as the stations failed to get even basic necessities to the ship. On September 16th, three DJs decided that enough was enough and they simply deserted the ship; Jonell, Charlie Wolf and Tommy Rivers all decided to quit together and sailed back to the UK in the early hours of the morning. They hitched a ride on a fishing boat to Ramsgate, choosing to avoid the station's regular port on the Isle of Sheppey.

Their departure left only two disc jockeys on board: Craig Novack and Chris Carson plus some recordings of Tommy, Jonell and Charlie which were hurriedly assembled to make up fresh sounding programmes. These were aired over the next few days in an attempt to trick the DTI to assume that all was still normal on board and not to mount a raid on the usual tender destination.

Charlie The Sea Wolf

Charlie Wolf told the Evening Standard "Morale on board has been very low the last few weeks and we have all had enough. Five of us have quit this week, two were already on shore leave but none of us will be going back." He also told the Evening Standard that Laser 558 still owed him a considerable amount of back pay and said he was getting very disenchanted by the lack of organisation and shore support.

Charlie claimed that he was being followed everywhere by the DTI and that hoped to at least pick up an air ticket from the station's manager, John Catlett. "I'm really sad to be leaving Laser," he professed. "It's a great station and I've had some wonderful times there, but the station never seems to be able to generate enough cash. The supply situation is just abysmal and it just isn't any fun any more."

Tommy Rivers said that the situation on board the ship had grown unworkable. "It's now just got horrible, there has been no fresh water on the ship for five weeks. None of us has been able to wash for many weeks now and it's been very tough on the girls." Tommy said that he felt that surviving the blockade for next two months was vital for Laser, as after that, everyone was pretty certain the DTI would be forced to retire for the winter. Tommy's words were very close to the mark; the winter weather was soon to have quite an effect in the Knock Deep, and the DTI were about to close down their operation there, calling the spy boat back to England.

After leaving Laser, Tommy married an English girl and then returned to the USA in 1986 where he joined KSTP 1500. Within a few years he was back in London working for United Press International. He then moved to NBC and to CBS, both as a London correspondent.

In 1993 Tommy joined *Virgin Radio*, then newly launched as the UK's third national radio station. Virgin broadcast rock music on 1214 kHz Medium Wave, the frequency originally used by BBC Radio One when it launched. Tommy hosted weekend shows for the station for two years, but now works for ABC News Radio, again as the network's London correspondent.

A few days later a new voice was to be heard on Laser 558, **Jay Mack**, a DJ from Boston, Massachusetts. It wasn't the original legendary Jay Mack of course, who a very well known American DJ, but a former student from Boulder, Colorado.

He had became interested in pirate radio when he toured the Netherlands in 1970, Ten years later, while working at a station in Massachusetts, he met Craig Novak. When Craig later joined Laser he suggested to John Catlett that Jay would be a good DJ signing.

Jay had a baptism of fire getting to the ship too. While he was climbing aboard from the tender the Dioptric Surveyor pulled alongside and bathed him with its powerful searchlight. For the next six weeks he worked some very long shifts; five or six hour shifts were now becoming routine on Laser due to the lack of staff.

The last few days of September brought urgent appeals on the air for food to be taken out to the ship. Radio Caroline sent them over a boat of food, which was traded for some fresh water as the Ross Revenge was low on it. There were frequent trips between the two radio ships and many DJs spent the night on their rival's boat, just to get a break. All except LiZ West: "Liz thought the guys on Caroline were very unprofessional and always stayed on the Communicator," confirmed Mike Barrington, who worked on both ships.

A further call for food was answered at the end of September by the tender bringing out another new DJ **Chuck Cannon**, from San Francisco in California. He had studied radio at San Mateo and worked at several stations in San Diego, Phoenix and in San Bernardino before arriving on the Communicator. Chuck was to stay with Laser 558 until the station closed.

It was at this time that the latest publicity stunt was released on the public – a commercial recording of a track the station had been playing for some weeks. The disco hit *I Spy for the FBI*, had been re-recorded by some members of the bands 'Sad Café' and 'Boys Don't Cry' as well as John Wilson and Paul Young Two of Laser's DJ team Liz West and Erin Kelly could also be heard on it. An energetic up-tempo song it poked fun at the Whitehall servants charged with  monitoring the station. One of the Laser 558 Road Show presenters, Robbie Day, was featured rapping on the record. It was at their well-attended gigs where he and the other team members would mime to the record as it was played.

After hearing rumours that the British Government were trying to get the ship's registration withdrawn by Panama, Tom de Munck, a well known Dutch radio journalist, called the Panamanian Shipping Registration office in New York to find out more. They told him that a procedure to achieve this had already started a couple of months ago. The UK had been lodging complaints with Panama's government since 1984 but these had been ignored by officials until diplomatic pressure was brought to bear.

 When John Catlett was quizzed about the registration problems, he told the reporters that he was not aware of it at all. "The lawyer responsible for all matters concerning the Communicator, Glenn Kolk in Miami, is not available for comment; even I can't get hold of him."

The Panamanian shipping bureau was a lot more forthcoming; they were happy to confirm that the matter of deregistration would be completed within the next two weeks. They said that the ship's owners had been difficult to contact and they had exhausted all channels.

If the Communicator was left without a flag at sea, it could be boarded by the British authorities or anyone who wished to take command of the ship. Security on board was very lax with no proper watch being maintained quite often. The crew would still not allow visitors to have access to some areas however, which led to some unfortunate rumours about other activities taking place on the ship. These were probably untrue, but strict adherence to petty rules only served to fuel all kinds of gossip.

Charlie Wolf's decision to leave the ship at the same time as Tommy and Jonell had come after the supply situation started to grow worse. This left only Chris Carson and Craig Novak on board and they were reduced to playing pre-recorded tapes as they were unable to sustain the long hours of broadcasting.

In an interview with Offshore Echos magazine the following month, Charlie Wolf commented, "We actually did change the face of radio. Johnny Beerling, then the Controller of BBC Radio One, told me so. He said that we forced through the changes at Radio One and he believed, at many other stations too. We kicked British radio in the backside and it would be nice to kick them in the backside again as they need it. Even more so now, they really do!"

More damage to the antenna occurred in another bout of heavy weather that put the station off the air for another four days at the beginning of October. During that time Chris Carson, the last remaining female DJ on board, left the station. She flew immediately back to the USA and joined station KVLT in Tulsa, Oklahoma.

Chris was replaced by **John Leeds,** who was very soon to make the last announcement on the station before it closed for good. He was a Texan who had been working at KITE, a Contemporary Hit 40 station in Corpus Christi, not far from the Mexican border, out on the Gulf. He returned to Texas after he left Laser just a month later and joined KEYS 1440, a Gold station, then enrolled at the University of Houston. After a few more radio gigs he started his own photography business and has since become a Minister, specialising in mixed faith ceremonies.

In early October, Laser 558 was often off the air as one generator after another broke down, leaving the ship without any power for lengthy periods. The main power units were a General Motors 60 Hz model with a Detroit Diesels motor, and an Alice Chalmers combo that had been installed in New Ross in Ireland. It had previously seen only standby use at a hospital in Kent, with only 80 hours 'on the clock'.

These two large units were augmented by a Lister 6 cylinder, 65-HP set that was enough to run one transmitter. It was one of the most reliable rigs on the ship, but all three were excellent workhorses. So long as their oil and filters were changed about every other week, they would have given valiant service for maybe ten or fifteen years, maybe more.

One of the biggest problems during the last month of Laser 558 was the chronically low level of fuel. When the levels in the Communicator's fuel tanks ran very low, dirt that had settled to the bottom was sucked up into the intakes and had to be laboriously cleaned from the generators' injectors by hand. Low fuel levels also resulted in water pooling in one tank, caused by condensation, which also affected the running of the generators.

Although redundancy had been built into the installation by having extra generators, these had not been well maintained and one by one they all spent longer and longer offline. The usual reasons for the generators being inoperable were the lack of spare parts on the ship and the delays in getting replacements. The harsh conditions encountered at sea meant that seawater often reached delicate components in the alternator part of the generator, but these were often the most reliable part of the installation. The generators were originally set for 12 wire, 'High Y' connection and their output was three phase, 440 volt.

Routine maintenance, such as oil filter cleaning and regular temperature checks, plus the really important things, like oil changes, all were left undone from week to week. The injectors on large diesel engines could be cleaned reasonably well with clean diesel and parafin. The big difficulty was that this would have meant taking the generator off line (out of service) for a few hours, perhaps a day. But the biggest problem there was no one to do the work!

The Detroit Diesels generator "in bits" (with its alternator removed)

There was often no standby power supply source to allow the station to stay on the air while these routine jobs were accomplished. Often there was no experienced fitter on board able to do the job. Anyone at Radio Caroline could have told Laser's management that this was work that could not be scrimped on.

This invariably meant that when the engine finally gave up it was a major component that would fail, such as con-rods, or shell bearing, which meant major surgery to get them running again. Ever more specialised tools were needed, a larger inventory of spare parts and of course the experienced manpower to do the work.

It was evident that the DTI blockade was beginning to work, with the lack of any tenders from Spain and its reliance on obtaining supplies from the UK exposing flaws in Laser's organisation. Radio Caroline transmissions continued uninterrupted, thanks to the Zeemeeuw from Nieuwpoort in Belgium and a Honduran registered vessel called the MV Windy running supplies. Both tenders had experienced skippers who also ran trips for radio fans to visit the radio ships, but being registered in Honduras, the British Authorities on the DTI spy boat could not stop them making deliveries.

Further breakdowns on the last remaining generator took Laser 558 off the air again a few days later. Even the disc based Scott Shannon seemed to have left Laser one weekend but he was genuinely on holiday and his American Top 40 show was hosted by **Shadoe Stevens**, a well known DJ in the USA. He began broadcasting from a homemade transmitter in the attic of his home in North Dakota, before joining a long list of stations. A few years after his 'trial' show on Laser, Shadoe took over Scott Shannon's American Top 40 show.

Copies of the *I Spy for the DTI* parody song were now on general release in record shops, but it got no airplay from any other radio stations. The label said it was made at CIA Studios in Washington by the *The Moronic Surveyors!*

Another main power generator – the Allis Chalmers set.

by Leendert Vingerling

A few days later yet another new DJ stepped on to the Communicator to present programmes live. **Jeff Davis** (seen below with Chuck Cannon) was a native of St Louis in Missouri where had trained at the Broadcast Centre. When Jeff's parents moved to Tucson in Arizona Jeff moved with them.

Within weeks of his 18th birthday he got a job at KRQ 93, where he had worked with Blake Williams, who joined Laser in December 1983. Jeff racked up about seven years experience at various stations in Arizona, quite a different environment to the now increasingly hostile North Sea. After leaving Radio Caroline, Blake had visited his folks in Arizona for a while, en route to Guam and he shared his stories and photographs of life on the Communicator

Laser 558 DJs Chuck Cannon and Jeff Davis.

Jeff was sufficiently intrigued to apply for a job and John Catlett flew to Phoenix to meet with him and sign him up. Jeff met up with John Leeds at Newark, NJ, airport to fly across the Atlantic and all went well until he reached Immigration at London Gatwick. As is normal he was asked how much cash he had with him; it's a standard question, to ensure countries don't let in anyone who hasn't enough money to support himself or herself.

Jeff lied at first saying he had $2,000 but it was in his checked baggage, hoping to bluff his way through the situation. The officer called his bluff and asked to see the money, so Jeff had no alternative but to 'come clean' and tell them what he was doing. He explained that he would be on his way out to the radio ship. Unfortunately the DTI had alerted the Immigration officers at Gatwick to be on the look out for Laser staff coming from the Virgin flight and the Immigration officers had to deport him, back to New Jersey on the next plane.

Laser management then arranged for Jeff to fly to Amsterdam where he was met by Radio Caroline's friends, Leendert and Marjo Vingerling. Due to the very rough weather at that time, there were no tenders running and Jeff had to stay with Marjo and Leendert in the Netherlands. His first need was for a winter coat as he had just arrived from Arizona, where people don't need them.

Jeff had a wonderful time in the Netherlands and has since returned to Europe to visit the Vingerlings with whom he became good friends. His journey out to the Communicator was to prove to be both lengthy and arduous.

It was to be over a week before the weather subsided; and first they had to drive down through Belgium to the port of departure, for the boat trip Jeff had been rescheduled onto was taking sightseers from Nieuwpoort. It was a long trip on the *MV Zeemeeuw* across to the Thames estuary, with a party of radio listeners.

When finally within sight of the MV Communicator, they then had to first tie up at Radio Caroline's ship, The Ross Revenge, for a few hours sightseeing before sailing the last two miles to the Communicator. Most of the radio enthusiasts had not been aware that they had a real live Laser DJ in their midst!

The final Laser 558 DJ line up: Craig, Chuck, Jay, John and Jeff

In mid October the DTI staged a road show of their own, inviting carefully selected journalists to hear officialdom's side of the story. It was presented by a very cold, Whitehall apparatchik called Dillys Gane. She trotted out all the usual allegations of interference and a danger to health and safety, all of which had been resolutely rebutted many times already by sailors and radio experts. The DTI were now advised by their lawyers to add caveats and cop-outs such as 'potentially' and 'could have' to their claims.

Ms Gane told the press that their observation ship, the Dioptric Surveyor, had often cruised close by the two radio ships in the Knock Deep and had observed seventeen vessels making supply runs in the two months since August. Seventeen is a total to which many Laser DJs would only comment – "The DTI are either nuts, blind or simply liars. We really do wish we had seen 17 supply boats, or even half that number!"

The DTI were now circling the Communicator very closely every couple of hours which was very disconcerting for new members of the team who had just joined. At night the ship was frequently buzzed by a helicopter from the nearby RAF Manston with a powerful searchlight. Towards the end of October, the DJs stopped referring to the DTI but the presence was intensified and the close up visits ever more frequent. The DTI never attempted to board the Communicator, but would come by very close and very often.

There are well-established rules for ships at sea and the proximity of other vehicle. The DTI flouted flag signals flown from the Communicator, knowing that some of the signals flown, such as "I have divers down, stay away" were false. They also ignored the principles of which side another boat may be passed on and on the sounding of audible horns. DTI spies on board the Dioptric Surveyor would point a variety of lenses at anything and anyone out on the deck of the Communicator. They would also try to take photographs through the portholes, giving a firm and clear message that they were still very much in the Knock Deep, keeping watch.

The DTI couldn't stop foreign vessels getting through however; one delivered around 500 gallons of diesel to th Communicator on the 20th October. This would normally last two weeks, however Laser remained silent, thanks to a generator breakdown and there being noone on board capable of fixing it. Foreign tender operators had offered to take supplies to and from the Communicator several times but Laser management always refused, as all their supplies were being handled by Estuary Tugs on the Isle of Sheppey.

Towards the end of October 1985 things on the Communicator were getting really desperate, as the British tug would not take out further supplies. In desperation, John Catlett called Leendert Vingerling in Holland to ask him to get some supplies to the Communicator. Sensing that the problem with the UK supplier was not only the spy boat's presence, but also the tardiness of payments, Leendert insisted on being paid in advance by Laser. He knew that tender runs done on credit were often not paid quickly, but still the tender costs of crew wages, fuel and the running costs must be paid for. Funds were not forthcoming from Laser so no supplies were taken out at that time.

The next day, regional ITV station TVS ran the interview that they had conducted with Liz West at the small B&B in Rochester where she had been marooned since leaving the ship. Liz told viewers how the Communicator crew often went for several weeks without fresh food or water and that conditions on board were simply horrendous. She was owed several thousands of pounds in wages and had been left penniless. Apart from a free holiday in Morocco she had not received any pay for the seven months she had worked for the station.

Liz told viewers how she had been working for two very long periods on the ship without a break and said that she had been on board the Communicator for a tour of fourteen weeks and then later for ten weeks during which she had contracted a severe bout of dysentery. In a full and frank interview she said "We have not been paid for weeks and the ship isn't even being supplied properly with food. There are no female sanitary products on board and we just feel totally abandoned out there. I certainly will not be going back."

Liz claimed the company had failed to get her any medical help or transfer her to shore when she was dangerously ill, despite this being quite legal under the Marine Offences Act as her health was in danger. "The Captain thought I had scurvy because I had eaten no fresh vegetables for so long; we had no fresh water and the milk had run out. There wasn't even any toilet paper on board the ship for at least three weeks."

During the last few days of October, the British Government confirmed that they were taking steps to have the registration for the Communicator cancelled. It would be unable to apply for a flag from any other country as its safety certificates had now expired which needed a visit to a harbour for renewal.

I Spy for the DTI was finally making some headway in the record sales charts; many local newspapers reported healthy sales of it in their local areas, especially in the southeast. Laser's chart had the song at number 14, and it now included the line "100,000 bucks a month to bring Laser to its knees" supposedly spoken by a DTI man from Whitehall, but in reality this was voiced Road Show DJ, Rob Day.

The DTI's original claim of investing £50,00 a month into the surveillance had now been revised to be only £25,000 a month. A local newspaper in Kent reported at the end of October that its own investigation into the DTI claims of widespread interference had found no evidence of any danger. Their reporter, John Webster, had spoken to Dover Coastguard and to two pilots of the helicopters at RAF Manston, one of whom said "We have never had any problems of interference from either Laser or Caroline with any of our frequencies." The RAF routinely log incidents of interference, for training and as evidence for investigations, but no trace was found to support the DTI's claim.

Coastguard staff at their main Dover control centre said, "We have not had any problems whatsoever, it must be another country's coastguards that the DTI are referring to as it certainly isn't us." In fact the coastguards use VHF frequencies around 160MHz to communicate with shipping and their own team. Use by any coast stations of the old MF bands had almost died out by then.

Lightships used a few spot frequencies around 2,000 kHz but this was almost four times the 558 frequency used by Laser. Trinity House operate the lightships around England and their records show that the last time there was any 'interference' by a radio ship was 15 years previously. In 1970, Radio North Sea International could be briefly and intermittently heard on one frequency, but this was later found to be due to maladjusted equipment at Walton coastguard station.

These claims had been the mainstay of the DTI's campaign. The DTI also claimed that "Laser blasts the medium wave band with 50,000 watts of power." This statement was disingenuous at best, but perhaps a little closer to a downright lie; the highest power that Laser 558 had been able to manage so far was 12,000 watts and it had recently been running around 6 kilowatts.

The first of November dawned grey and grizzly on the North Sea and Radio Caroline's breakfast DJ Nick Richards thought he was seeing double when he looked out of his porthole; not only could he see one Communicator, but what looked like two of them! In fact it was a sister ship of the Communicator, the Gardline Tracker. Very similar in size and shape and with the same colour scheme, it differed only in missing a pair of tall masts. Was this the much rumoured third radio ship that had suddenly appeared in the Knock Deep?

Any hopes that the new ship might be a friendly new neighbour were soon dashed when it was revealed to be yet another spy ship, chartered by the DTI. The Gardline Tracker was indeed a former sister ship of the Communicator, that was taking over from the Dioptric Surveyor.

Chartered from Gardline Surveys Limited of Lowestoft, Suffolk, the Tracker was a fine ship having also been built in 1953 by the same shipbuilder near Bremen in West Germany. Just ten feet shorter than the Communicator and of similar construction, she was much more suited to staying at sea in inclement weather than the Dioptric Surveyor, which was little more than a launch. The Tracker had operated in the North Atlantic like her sister and had an excellent crew of experienced seamen who could remain at sea all winter if necessary.

News of her arrival in the Knock Deep was met with dismay. The Laser team had hoped that the onset of winter and the expiration of the Dioptric Surveyor's contract might mean the end of Euroseige. Drafting in a large ship like the Gardline Tracker clearly meant that the siege would continue. Some small boats might be persuaded to 'beat the blockade' and run supplies or people out for pleasure in the calm summer months, but doing so in winter was not so easy. Fourteen miles from the nearest land and having to take the long way round to avoid sandbanks was no fun in bad weather and heavy seas.

The situation on board the Communicator was getting very bad with fresh food and water being in short supply; the lack of fuel made things more desperate. Spare parts were needed for a lot of the equipment, especially generators, which were essential to broadcast and to live.

Gardline Tracker joined the DTI's Eurosiege in November

Meanwhile on board the Communicator a huge row was taking place as Captain Pat Paternoster wanted to sail the ship into a port so he could relinquish his command. He and some of the crew were unhappy that their office was ignoring them and not sending out fresh supplies. The reason for the absence of a supply tender was simply that Laser had run out of money. The argument developed into a near mutiny and at one stage John Leeds called up Walton Coastguard by VHF and requested them to save him from the ship but they said that they were unable to help.

A drama occurred near the ship on the 4th of November when a small boat, the MV Windy, got a rope entangled in its propeller. The Windy was a Honduran registered supply boat, part manned by Cape Verde crew; she was now disabled, unable to use her propeller. Because it was November the sea temperature was so cold that there was no possibility of the crew going into the water to free the rope, so the DTI had to render assistance. With assistance from the Walton lifeboat the Windy was towed into Harwich for repairs.

A sailor climbs onto the Windy after crossing by dingy from a radio ship.
(In rough seas this was safer than having the boats alongside each other.)
by Fred Bolland

11. TO HARWICH FOR THE WINTER

The following morning, on Guy Fawkes Day, normal programmes on 558 kHz commenced but some real fireworks were about to fly. Craig Novack hosted the Laser breakfast programme and just after 8am he broadcast coded information asking for management to contact the ship urgently about the generators. It was repeated every fifteen minutes and laced with unbridled sarcasm, such as "if anyone is interested".

One of the last remaining operable generators had a serious fault and the crew could only continue generating power by hand pumping oil through it. John Leeds continued the messages to the shore base throughout the morning but no response was heard from the on shore team. Craig and the Captain decided to bring the Communicator in, as they didn't feel safe. Just after 12 o'clock midday the programme stopped and the transmitter was switched off a minute later. The main generator used to power the radio station had failed and the ship fell silent.

An engineer on Radio Caroline, Mike Barrington, had been speaking to the Communicator's captain over VHF radio and he had given advice to his neighbours on how to get the generators running again. This involved swapping components around but the Communicator had no competent diesel fitter or any kind of any engineer on board who could manage anything technical at all.

"It was infuriating to know that they had all they needed on board, they just needed an engineer to keep it going, or at least stayed at sea and been safe. We knew that there were supplies coming to them from France and that a tender was imminent to replenish the ship but her Captain wouldn't wait. He just wanted to get off. "

"Some of the DJ team were new and none had been out long enough to get used to the ways things had to be done on a radio ship," said Mike. "It's vital that a radio ship be kept out at sea as it can open a whole can of worms once you come into the UK."

Sister ships sailing in together
Gardline Tracker and the Communicator

The crew and the DJs were very dispirited due to the lack of contact and assistance from their own office and on shore staff. An urgent council of war was held by the crew and Captain Paternoster, decided he would take the Communicator into port, for the safety of his crew. He requested assistance from the DTI spy ship.

Engineers from the spy ship, the Gardline Tracker, were very familiar with the plant on the Communicator, some of them had worked on it until Gardline sold her to Laser, and they soon had the main engine running. The Tracker then escorted the Communicator from the Knock Deep, past the Radio Caroline ship, the Ross Revenge, whose crew watched aghast as the two sister ships sailed very slowly northwards, towards the port of Harwich.

"We watched as she slowly passed us, accompanied by the Gardline Tracker," remembers Mike Barrington. "We knew it was the end as I had been in touch by VHF radio most of the morning trying to help them sort their generators out. I had worked on there recently and knew where all the tanks and pipes were interconnected. The problem on the Communicator for a long time had been that they had no one who could do any engineering work at all, they couldn't even get the toilets flushing. They just were not organised on shore and had a very unreliable reputation for payment, feeding the crew and just generally getting things together."

""It was such a very sad day," said Leendert Vingerling who was on board the Ross Revenge that day and took the picture below as the Communicator sailed in. "It felt just as though a member of our family had died."

**Communicator steams past the Ross Revenge
On her way in to Harwich** (by Leendert Vingerling)

A Harwich pilot was put on board for the last few miles inbound, which is a requirement for any foreign ship entering a port, for navigational reasons. The news that Communicator was coming in was quickly passed among radio people on ashore and within an hour, one creditor of the station (me) had briefed lawyers to meet the ship in and affix a writ to have the ship arrested for the debts before it could be sailed back out to sea again. The Admiralty Marshall, Vincent Ricks, was briefed and he attended the ship when she arrived in Harwich at teatime on the 5th.

When she reached the harbour the Communicator was met by a phalanx of men from the Essex Police, the DTI, HM Customs and Immigration officials. She was moored just off the Parkestone Quay and an official boat took out approved visitors, including Laser's General Manager John Catlett.

In interviews with TVS, Anglia and other media, Catlett confessed that he didn't know what future there was for the station, or if it even had any future. He denied that the station had any debts and it was this statement that forced the imposition of the liens on the ship pending the outcome of court action.

Asked why the ship had needed to put into port, Catlett put the blame squarely at the feet of the ship's captain, saying that any other person would have repaired the equipment himself. Catlett claimed that by not doing so, Captain Paternoster he had scuppered Laser's chances of survival.

The seven Americans on board when the ship came into Harwich were allowed to remain on board overnight and then the following morning taken ashore to be interviewed by immigration officers. Each were given a Tourist Visa for thirty days and asked for their autographs for the Immigration Officers' families and friends! They were all taken to the company's usual hotel in Rochester for a couple of days before flying home to the USA. The four Britons on the crew were reported to the DPP by the DTI and then freed.

The ship however had to undergo a series of inspections by Board of Trade officials. They found a long list of faults and deficiencies that had to be remedied before the ship could go back to sea again. There was the small matter of a couple of writs for outstanding debts. The ship urgently needed £40,000 to pay off the immediate debts and to be fuelled and provisioned.

Paul Rusling's lawyer had the Admiralty Marshall stick a writ on the wheelhouse door and the Harwich Harbour Master announced that no one was to move the vessel until the disputed amounts were settled. The writ was signed and sealed and the ship ordered to remain moored on the River Stour. A further writ for other debts was added on the 2nd January

Government appointed ship keepers remained on board the MV Communicator, keeping guard. Paul Rusling's debt of over £7,000 had already been filed by his solicitor with the Admiralty Marshall, while the ship was still on her way into port. Papers were sworn in court on the same afternoon as she was nearing Harwich and now she would only be allowed to sail by depositing funds to cover the debt.

Several more creditors were expected to appear at the harbour over the next few days, as Laser seemed to owe so many people money In the event, many suppliers and former staff appeared to be afraid to present themselves to file a claim, fearing action from the DTI.

Norwich Eastern Daily Press reported that Great Yarmouth survey firm Gardline Shipping was drawing up a writ to serve on the MV Communicator. The managing director of Gardline, Mr George Darling, claimed they were owed £5,000 from September 1983 when the ship was originally sold to an American company. George Darling was convinced that the outstanding money would be collected and that the MV Communicator might sail under the Gardline flag once again!

The matter was discussed in the House of Commons two weeks later when Eric Forth, the MP for Worcestershire, asked the Secretary of State for Trade and Industry if he will give the circumstances surrounding the actions taken with regard to the Laser 558 radio station, and the statutory basis for such actions.

Mr Butcher who was at that time an Under-Secretary for the Department of Trade, responded: "The Department of Trade and Industry chartered a survey vessel on 8 August to observe supply traffic to the two marine broadcasting stations operating off the Essex coast. Evidence of a considerable number of possible offences has already been passed to the police both in the United Kingdom and in continental countries. Decisions on the prosecutions of UK nationals for offences against the Marine Etc. Broadcasting (Offences) Act will be made by the Director of Public Prosecutions."

"On the 6th of November, the vessel Communicator, from which Laser 558 broadcasts had been made, sailed to Harwich harbour following a generator breakdown" he continued. "The Communicator requested and received escort assistance from the DTI's chartered vessel. I understand that the Communicator is at present under the control of the Admiralty Marshal following legal action by an individual (Paul Rusling) and a private company (Gardline Shipping).

Mr Butcher informed the House that "the costs of the Department's surveillance operation in the North Sea are around £25,000 per month, including the costs of charter and staff costs. The operation has been directed against both Radio Caroline and Radio Laser 558."

Rusling's writ proceeded quickly through the system and the first hearing took place at the High Court on The Strand on the 14th December. The Admiralty Marshall reported that the scrap value of the ship Communicator was only £8,000 but that he had been told by the owner's representative she was worth over £1 million with all the equipment on board.

The DTI however were not happy at all with the prospect of the Communicator getting new owners and warned that if the ship were sold for broadcasting then they may consider prosecuting the Admiralty Marshall. Rusling's lawyer said that a simple condition to the sale might be added to any sale preventing the ship's use as a radio station again. This would enable a sale to go ahead and its debts to be cleared.

DTI ad in the music press

Another DTI waste of money appeared in the press in December, warning that British subjects could not advertise on offshore radio stations. Their bumbling meant it only appeared after Laser 558 had closed and the DTI had ended their surveillance of the remaining offshore broadcaster, Radio Caroline.

LEGAL NOTE

At no time did the British Government vessels attempt to board either of the radio ships or interfere with crew members during the blockade. Its purpose was simply to identify who was supplying the ships. Where the visitors were genuine foreign-registered vessels, various international treaties prevented the British Government from acting. Where supplies were being run out from the UK, the DTI's spy boat followed them back into the UK and attempted to obtain evidence for any subsequent prosecution.

Even while in Harwich harbour the Communicator managed to attract a fair share of controversy and drama, despite the Admiralty Marshall having engaged ship watchers to guard the vessel. They were not very observant and failed to notice visitors who climbed on board on at least two occasions to remove valuable radio components from the vessel.

Shortly after the Communicator came into port, the new spy ship Gardline Tracker suddenly disappeared from the Thames Estuary and the DTI confirmed that they had now completed their surveillance exercise. They did not intend resuming the exercise and Radio Caroline could continue at sea, as she had done previously. It was clear that the Communicator was the 'thorn in the side' and the real reason for Euroseige.

In fact the main reason a blockade on Radio Caroline was unnecessary was that its bulk supplies (food, fuel and water) were clearly coming from foreign registered boats sailing from the continent, over which the DTI had no powers while the ship remained in international waters. Its programmes were not outrageously successful, so it was no threat to the ILR stations in the UK.

Radio Caroline played down its UK presence and claimed to be international. Its London office was low key and while everyone knew who its owner and leader was, activities were covert and not rubbed in the Government's faces. By contrast, Laser was embarrassing UK radio with its success. It had a well known sales office operation in the West End of London, had persistently lied about its ownership and made no secret that its supplies came from the UK.

Laser DJ Charlie Wolf remained close to the Communicator after she sailed in and took a relief job at Radio Orwell, the ILR station in Ipswich. He was a little more subdued than he would no doubt have been onboard the Communicator, his true spiritual home. Along with Liz West (still kicking her heels, in Kent) they remained the only Laser DJs to have stayed in the UK, Tommy, Chuck, Craig, Jay, John and Jeff all having returned to the USA.

During the night of the 16th of January 1986 the Harwich inshore lifeboat rescued the two night watchmen from the ship and then stood by the MV Communicator after the alarm was raised that the ship may be on fire. The emergency services found no fire on board the Communicator, but the now silent radio ship had a faulty boiler causing the smoke. Twenty-four firemen from Colchester and Harwich took part in the operation as well as a fire launch plus local police and ambulance services. There was no damage to the ship, or to any of the equipment.

12. MV COMMUNICATOR FOR SALE

The failure of the ship's owners to settle the debts meant that the vessel could be sold to recoup the money owed. Kellocks, a well-known firm of shipbrokers based in the City of London were retained to act on behalf of the Admiralty Marshall. Kellocks knew a lot about ships but nothing about radio equipment and so they asked Ray Anderson of East Anglian Productions to value the radio equipment and told interested parties that they were looking for a six-figure offer for the Communicator and radio station, complete.

EAP immediately called Paul Rusling, who had installed the equipment and asked him to help value the installation. He simply replied "So long as it covers the money owed, I would put a very low value on it. Chained up in harbour with the a detention order on her, she is theoretically worth only scrap value." A valuation report by Graham Booth, a ship's valuer in Kent, for EAP put her value at approximately £150,000, excluding all the broadcasting equipment.

The Admiralty Marshall formally put the vessel up for sale in March 1986. Notices were sent to ship brokers all over Europe and adverts placed in shipping publications, as well as the broadcast press. The advertisements simply described the Communicator as

MV Communicator (Panamanian flag) - Floating Radio Station (Laser 558)

which implied official acceptance that the ship was a legitimate business.

The sale documents issued by Kellocks listed the radio equipment and studio kit in the ship. The advertisement attracted a lot of interest from various parties and after several inspections by some of them, over a dozen offers were received when the bidding closed the following month on the 8th April. Most were around the £10,000 mark, one as low as £5,000 from a scrap dealer. Two of the bids were for £25,000 and but one was for a little bit more.

Radio enthusiasts and Frinton residents alike were amazed to read in the press in the middle of April that the well known radio firm **East Anglian Productions**, who had valued the Communicator for the sale were the successful bidders at auction. Most readers were even more astonished to learn that the successful bid was for only £35,000, although a condition to the sale was that she must not be used for illegal broadcasting. As it had now been off the air almost six months it could hardly be described as a 'going concern.'

"Now we have got the ship there are a number of options open to us," said EAP's Managing Director, Ray Anderson. He had been a keen offshore radio fan for years and said it was like a Christmas present to own such a remarkable piece of radio history as the Communicator. "I see the vessel as a business proposition, to make a profit. I never expected my bid to be successful as I expected it to go for a lot more."

Studio House, 21-23 Walton Road, Frinton-on-Sea, Essex, CO13 0AA, England
Telephone Frinton (025 56) 6252   Telex 987273 KIRBY

PRESS RELEASE

21 April, 1986

Radio Laser - m.v. Communicator

Frinton-on-Sea based East Anglian Productions has purchased the ex-Radio Laser radio ship the m.v. Communicator for £35,000 from the Admiralty Marshal following the collapse of the Radio Laser Company last November. The vessel had been under arrest in the Essex port of Harwich.

East Anglian Productions are a Frinton based communications company producing many regional TV and Radio Commercials, Corporate Video Productions and Broadcast Equipment Sales. Ironically, the company produced a documentary on Radio Laser filmed on board last September. The company's Managing Director Mr. Ray Anderson said that the £35,000 paid for the vessel represents a fraction of the ship's true worth. The vessel is equipped with 2 powerful 25 kilowatt AM transmitters, studios, generating plant and a sophisticated Satellite Communications system. As a working unit, Ray Anderson said that the true worth was closer to £250,000.

East Anglian Productions are now considering a number of legal options for future use of the vessel. One includes an outright sale to a consortium for possible use in the Mediterranean Sea, as a 'Summer only' - English speaking radio station for tourists. Also, an International film company is producing a 'Rock Music' film centred around the former offshore radio station and have expressed an interest in using the vessel on a hire basis. We are also expecting some interest from the various Free Radio Organisations who may wish to see the vessel turned into a museum. However, it is more likely that the vessel will be taken to another part of the world where it could very easily be used as a commercial radio station and operate quite legally.

"It's Ours" proclamation by EAP

East Anglian Productions and their Managing Director Ray Anderson were clearly delighted with their purchase. They now suddenly decided that the ship was in fact worth £250,000 and issued a Press Release (see above) only days after their windfall.

The Press Release also admitted that EAP didn't know what they would do with it and at one stage they suggested that they would probably put it straight back up for sale again ('flip' the asset as the Americans call it), but Mr Anderson was keen to assure reporters that it would not be used for illegal broadcasting.

He and his assistants, Paul McLaren and Dennis Jason, immediately set about the renovation work. They first ripped apart the former ship's bar below decks, taking out the light wood panelling and other fixtures, but leaving up the dartboard which had seen many hours of use by all the Laser DJs, many of whom had been introduced to the sport while there. The plan was to add about fifty tons of sand as extra ballast, in order to make the ship more stable.

The exterior of the ship was tidied and repainted a more cherry red colour than her previous 'international orange and rust' colour scheme! In an attempt to make her look longer, sleeker and more streamlined, a band of black paint was applied to the area around the upper level of the superstructure, around the crew's day areas including the mess rooms and galley.

Most of the rust streaks were only where supply boats rubbing alongside had scraped off the paint. Best marine practice was, in the absence of bespoke rubber fenders, to hang old truck tyres over the side to prevent this abrasion however, there never seemed to be enough old tyres out at sea!

MV Communicator with her smart new paintwork of a black band.

Next the EAP army of workers converted a former ship's mess into a more comfortable room with sofas and a TV. The ship's main food storage area had an extra four large chest freezers installed which EAP thought would be sufficient to last the crew for three months.

A lot of the studio equipment was removed for restoration and upgrading, including the studio mixers and the playout cart machines. The two CSI transmitters remained on board however, being about the size of a domestic bathroom they were not easy to remove and any necessary work on them was done while they remained 'in situ'.

The power generators were slowly brought back into use. They needed a lot of work as neglect during 1985 and various 'bodges' using the wrong spare parts had taken its toll on some of them. They were soon brought back into operation, largely with the help of experienced engineer Mike Barrington, who had now been lured across from the Ross Revenge.

A lot of hard work was done over the next few weeks with Mike Barrington even managing to get the Communicator's 'reverse osmosis' water treatment plant working. This contraption, bought by the two Pauls in Florida, took raw seawater in and turned it into drinking water. This was one of the key items that would make life so much more bearable on a radio ship for the crew, fresh water; at one stage a spare unit was going to be installed. All it had needed was the correct filters and someone willing to read the instruction manual!

**Ray Anderson, MD of East Anglian Productions
pondering what to do with his new toy**

Over the summer, several groups of prospective buyers went on board the Communicator to assess the ship's possible use. Among these was a group of entrepreneurs who wanted to use the ship off Lanzarote for a new radio station broadcasting to the Canary Islands

Paul Rusling had been working with other radio station operators at the time, one of whom was hatching plans to launch another new station from a ship in the Thames estuary with an AM Stereo signal. The backers of that station had a ship, transmitters and even a 240 feet tall radio mast nearing completion in Santander, a large port in Northern Spain, by that stage.

The mast on the MV Nannell had been built at an engineering factory in Kent in some secrecy but DTI Investigators were tipped off by a Radio Caroline employee and they raided the fabricating yard. The surprised workers there told them that the structures they were working on were new lighting pylons for Southend Football Club and they were incomplete.

By the time the DTI had investigated further and returned to 'arrest' the mast, it was gone! It had been mysteriously been spirited away during the night to be hidden in London and then taken down to Plymouth docks. Due to its huge size, at one stage of the journey it even had a police escort! It was then taken by ferry to Santander on the northern coast of Spain's to be fitted onto the ship, which had meanwhile slipped out from Southampton and across the Bay of Biscay.

MV Nannell with its 240-foot mast, telescoped down and awaiting guying.

The new radio station that was to broadcast from the MV Nannell in AM Stereo was to be called *Stereo Hits 531*, using a surprisingly clear frequency at the very start of the Medium Wave band. At that time it was only in use irregularly and at low power in the Faroe Islands. It was then mooted that rather than await their own ship to be fitted, the Stereo Hits project would put in a bid for the Communicator. Only failure to submit the correct papers stopped them from acquiring the Communicator, otherwise we would have been adding Stereo Hits 531 to the list of stations broadcasting from the ship.

The usual greed and an element of thuggery had driven some of the key team members away from the Stereo Hits 531 project, which then managed to lose its magnificent 240 feet lattice mast in the Bay of Biscay. Undeterred, the owners had it towed up to the Belgian coast where it spent some months becalmed, making only a few short test transmissions on FM before being scrapped.

Talks were also held with Ronan O'Rahilly, of Radio Caroline, whose ship was keen to buy a high power transmitter for its 558 Service, however they failed to assemble a credible corporate vehicle (a legally constituted company) to make a firm bid in time for the closing date.

EAP felt there was a future in the Communicator recommencing broadcasts and they immediately began plans to refloat the station. Work was begun in earnest, making the necessary repairs to the ship and it wasn't long before the rumour mill lumbered into action. EAP had hired some former Radio Caroline staff to get the Communicator back to sea again and it wasn't long before this came to the attention of the authorities.

"We get lots of visitors coming out to look at the ship, especially at weekends," said Ray Anderson. "Most come by in speedboats and from every direction, but we don't allow many on board as it could disrupt the renovation work on the ship."

Work was going ahead to remedy deficiencies found in the DoT's inspection. Local firm *R&J Marine Electronics* of Dovercourt tested all the ship's radio equipment on the 11th of September and found the Satellite installation, the VHF and MF equipment all in perfect working order. Only a small emergency transmitter in the lifeboat gave concern.

The DTI meanwhile were pressing their vendetta against the Communicator's crew in the courts. In early September the Communicator's captain who had brought her in, Pat Paternoster of Ipswich, appeared. He was charged with "carrying wireless telegraphy equipment which he knew would be used for illegal broadcasting."

Paternoster had already pleaded 'Not Guilty' at an earlier hearing and at this one his defence lawyer, Michael Lane, maintained that the case could not be brought as it discriminated against Mr Paternoster. He said that the Marine Offences Act of 1967 (under which the charge was brought) had been superseded by a European Union Treaty. As a member of the EU, the UK could not discriminate and that the court was obliged to take European community law into consideration. "English courts must give precedence and primacy to EEC law where there is any conflict between it and UK law," said Mr Lane. "The rights of the European Community must be extended to all British subjects. The court has no choice and must acquit the defendant."

The prosecution however maintained that the EEC Treaty was only designed to prevent member states from discriminating against foreigners and it was not designed to prevent action against a country's own nationals. After retiring for a lengthy period and consulting their advisers, the court found Captain Paternoster guilty and fined him £150.

The biggest court case in the history of offshore radio was set for hearing as summons were issued against fourteen people alleging a variety of offences, including "conspiracy to operate an offshore radio station".

Those facing court action included the owners of Estuary Tugs in the Isle of Sheppey, several concerned in signing up advertisers for the station, in obtaining music for the station and the publisher of a magazine who had run an article in praise of Laser.

Most were charged with conspiring to break the Marine Offences Act. Eventually all the charges were dropped as the DPP had used the wrong text in formulating the charges. Tony Elliott had his charges dropped and his magazine, Time Out, was charged instead, another charge later dropped.

On 26th September HM Custom officers disabled the MV Communicator by removing two of her drive shaft bearings. They took the action on behalf of the DTI, who had heard rumours that the ship was going to slip her moorings before she had been checked for seaworthiness. When it became publicly known that the ship had been disabled, the ship-breaking firm that was by now breaking up the Gardline Tracker (the MV Communicator's sister ship) offered to supply replacements free of charge, using parts from that vessel.

A spokesman for HM Customs said that it had been widely rumoured that the Communicator was about to slip back out to sea and they were concerned that some of the safety work, mandated by the inspection carried out when she came in the previous November, had not yet been completed. Ray Anderson of EAP protested and claimed that thousands of pounds had been invested in the ship to get her fit for sea. EAP's lawyers threatened legal action unless the engine parts were returned immediately.

The Harwich harbourmaster, Captain Ian Whale, commented "We don't like vessels to be immobilised in an anchorage, especially from a safety point of view, but when the Communicator broke adrift a few months ago it was tug assistance that saved her rather than her own engines."

Following another incident six weeks later the Communicator dragged her anchor again in the harbour during a gale. She almost hit the Sealink ship the Cambridge Ferry and had to be brought under control by a tug from Felixstowe. The Communicator was then tied up at Parkestone Quay, for the safety of all the ships in the harbour.

This was the fourth time the Communicator had dragged her anchors and twice ran aground, so in late October 1985 Mr Whale wrote to EAP with a Special Direction requiring them to take measures to adequately secure the ship. He suggested how this should be done with both the Communicator's bow anchors out and a heavy stern anchor. He said that as an alternative the ship should take a mud berth or go into an alongside berth, perhaps in Ipswich docks. Mr Whale said he had given the Special Direction to protect the safety of other shipping in Harwich harbour.

When questions were asked on the grounds of safety why the bearings had been removed, Mr DJ Feasey, the surveyor for HM Customs and Excise said the engine bearings had been removed on orders from the Department of Transport. Their own spokesman then responded, "That is nothing to do with us, the immobilisation of the engines is not our concern".

On 24th October however, without any prior notice, as message came from the Goivernment's legal department (believed to be the Attorney General no less!) to Harwich. Engineers and HM Customs officers boarded the MV Communicator in the River Stour and replaced the bearings that they had removed previously.

"All the safety improvements demanded of us have been carried out," said Ray Anderson. "The authorities were even accusing us of not carrying out safety improvements when in fact nobody from the department had visited the vessel since last November to check on progress. All we have to do now is get the Panamanian Authorities to issue certificates and then we should be able to get the Detention Order lifted from the vessel."|

EAP accused the DTI's Radio Regulatory Department, responsible for Euroseige 85, of stirring up the matter and then using the Department of Transport to cover up their action. The DTI had also been putting pressure on local companies, telling them that if they supplied the ship with any goods or services, they could be prosecuted under the Marine Offences Act.

A local newspaper quoted the MD of the Selixarc Tug Company as saying "The DTI advised us that if we supply fuel or any service to the MV Communicator knowing that it might be used as a pirate radio station, we could be left open to the risk of prosecution. Although I do not suspect it would be, I was not prepared to take the risk and we've stopped supplying fuel to the ship."

Work on getting the ship ready for broadcasting continued apace and was much easier now the ship that the Communicator was alongside and could be easily accessed from ashore. A stream of flunkeys could be seen carrying equipment onto the ship and supplies to fill the four new freezers installed down in the hold.

It seemed that a anice sheen had been put on the cosmetic aspects of the ship, but little seemed to have been done to the generators, the water system, the masts and aerials. This was to prove the downfall of the station.

In early November surveyors from the Panamanian Bureau of Shipping, led by their London Surveyor W.W. Martin, attended the ship and, after a thorough inspection, they pronounced that all the ship's equipment met their requirements. The surveyors issued the MV Communicator with new certification for Tonnage, Safety, Radiotelephony, MARPOL and Accommodation, at a cost of £4,250 which brought all the paperwork up to date.

Ray Anderson hoists the Panamanian flag

A few days later when the Department of Transport officials inspected the Communicator's now 'up to date and compliant' certification once again, they lifted the detention order which had been in place for just over a year. The ship was free to leave whenever her Captain wished.

That same day, EAP claimed that the ship and its radio contents had been sold to a foreign buyer, the *Cord Cabo Corporation of Panama*. Ray Anderson, the MD of EAP, told journalists that the ship was going to be delivered to her new owners off the coast of Gibraltar, and after that he expected her to be used for broadcasting somewhere in the Mediterranean. His lawyer, Les Livermore had dealt with all the paperwork relating to the sale and Ray told reporters that he didn't know precisely who the buyers were.

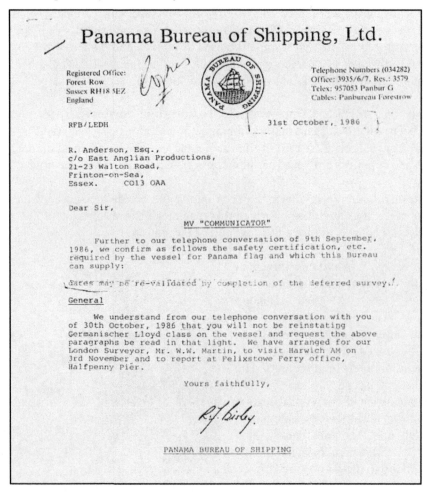

Panama Bureau of Shipping, Ltd.

Registered Office:
Forest Row
Sussex RH18 5EZ
England

Telephone Numbers (034282)
Office: 3935/6/7. Res.: 3579
Telex: 957053 Panbur G
Cables: Panbureau Forestrow

RFB/LEDH   31st October, 1986

R. Anderson, Esq.,
c/o East Anglian Productions,
21-23 Walton Road,
Frinton-on-Sea,
Essex.   CO13 OAA

Dear Sir,

                    MV "COMMUNICATOR"

    Further to our telephone conversation of 9th September,
1986, we confirm as follows the safety certification, etc.
required by the vessel for Panama flag and which this Bureau
can supply:

dates may be re-validated by completion of the deferred survey.

General

    We understand from our telephone conversation with you
of 30th October, 1986 that you will not be reinstating
Germanischer Lloyd class on the vessel and request the above
paragraphs be read in that light. We have arranged for our
London Surveyor, Mr. W.W. Martin, to visit Harwich AM on
3rd November and to report at Felixstowe Ferry office,
Halfpenny Pier.

                    Yours faithfully,

                    R.J. Birley.

          PANAMA BUREAU OF SHIPPING

Once she was 'sold' to a third party, it was impossible to enforce the covenant placed on the ship when she was sold by the Admiralty Marshall, that she must not be used for illegal broadcasting. The DTI were furious when they realised this but there was nothing they could do but stand and watch the ship sail, and listen to her resume broadcasting.

It was in the early hours of Sunday the 16th of November that the Communicator slipped her ropes at Parkestone Quay and headed back out to sea, after just over a year's incarceration. She was manned by only her Captain and half a dozen engineers. No DJs were in sight, although some of the engineers had often been heard on the air on Radio Caroline in the past.

The Communicator initially moored in the Cork anchorage near to Sealand, within sight of Felixstowe. This was to enable some further work on her antenna system. Crew members told contacts that they expected to be back on station in the Knock Deep in a few days.

Heading back out to sea in November 1986

13. LASER HOT HITS

A week later a press release was issued by Laser Hot Hits, of Suite 3600 on the 21st floor at 515 Madison Avenue in New York, the same building used by Laser 558 in her final months of operation, before she surrendered.

"Radio Laser is due to recommence transmissions of American format pop music from the MV Communicator anchored in the International Waters of the North Sea on Monday 1st December. The vessel has spent the last year in Harwich being refurbished by East Anglian Productions who purchased the vessel from the Admiralty Marshall following the collapse of the previous company.

The vessel was inspected by Department of Trade officials who cleared the vessel in mid November. The all-American deejays will present a formula of Hot Hits of European and American chart records, with selected oldies, 20 hours a day to an estimated 10 million listeners in the UK and the Continent. Ex Radio One Newsbeat newsreader Andrew Turner will present hourly news bulletins.

A Dallas based company **'Radio Waves International'** *have initial advertising contracts for $250,000 in the first three months of operation, including major American film and entertainment companies. International holiday companies, a leading Japanese car company and various sponsored programmes throughout the week. Radio Laser is also promoting her own anti-Drugs campaign with a £1,000,000 budget. An Aids campaign and a Christmas 'Drink Drive' campaign is also planned for later.*

All supplies to the vessel are being supplied by European legal routes; even duty free fuel, tobacco and spirits are being supplied by our tendering company. As the vessel is in International Waters the radio station is perfectly legal. The American DJs are not breaking "The Marine Offences Act of 1967" as it only applies to British subjects. All supplies are being supplied from the continent so as not to provoke the British authorities."

The date set for the relaunch of Laser was the 1st December and several newspaper articles locally and the trade press trumpeted the return to the airwaves of the station. Many people tuned around the dial to hear the station, but there wasn't a trace to be heard from the ship all day.

When the Laser Hot Hits reports appeared in national newspapers, such as the Daily Telegraph (who printed it almost word for word, in its entirety), a spokesman at East Anglian Productions said that he very much doubted that the ship would broadcast again in the North Sea. He said the ship was lying off Essex waiting for a delivery crew before steaming south, as far as he knew.

Finally as the dusk descended over the Thames estuary and the Communicator heaved and rolled in the increasing swell, the CSI transmitters were fired up once again. By 6pm the all-new 'Laser Hot Hits' could be heard on the ship's new frequency, 576 kHz.

by Paul Alexander Rusling

During test transmissions the new station was using lots of identifications voiced by **Bill Mitchell**, with his well-known deep gruff baritone voice, very familiar from other station identifications and many well-known TV commercials. His main announcement sounded awesome:

**Returning to your radio sets,
LASER IS BACK,
Bigger and Better than ever before**

**More powerful,
hot rocking and flame throwing
A new formula of HOT HITS,
recent hits & oldies.**

**Yes, LASER IS BACK
It's new, It's improved
And it's better than ever before**

**Programme details will be announced soon,
so go and tell a friend, - tell 'em LASER IS BACK
And stay tuned to this channel!**

Bill Mitchell

That was the text of Bill's announcements that were heard at the restart of transmissions from the Communicator. The DTI inspectors immediately contacted his agent, as he was a very high profile voice, well known for radio and TV commercials. "The Man in Black" was untouchable however as he was a Canadian citizen and without evidence that he had recorded the IDs in the UK there was nothing the DTI could do, even had he been British.

Shortly after teatime the blank carrier gave way to the old Laser closedown tune of Abba's *Thank you for the Music*, followed by a montage of jingles from many other offshore radio stations in whose steps the new station was treading.

At 9pm Laser Hot Hits had its big launch, with a new DJ **Johnny "Rock'n'Roll" Anthony**. He had a fast pacy style of delivery and what many thought was a style of presentation was long missing from the radio dial. It bode good things for the new Laser Hot Hits. Johnny was clearly very excited by the occasion and opened by thanking the ship's three engineers Johnny, Mike and James, for all their hard work.

The station continued with its special launch programme until midnight before closing for the night. John Anthony was in fine form and sounded really excited and ethusiastic on the newly relaunched LASER.

When the station reopened next morning John Anthony was still mike side and he explained that he was the only DJ on the ship at that point and was so exhausted after the launch day. He offered a new *Laser Hot Hits* T-Shirt for sale and promised listeners that if the station could sell a million of them, then they wouldn't need to run any commercials and Laser Hot Hits could then play even more music!

Johnny 'Rock'n'Roll' Anthony on the air at *Laser Hot Hits*.

The Communicator was not yet anchored in the Knock Deep channel but was further north, closer to Felixstowe, for several reasons. Later that morning the ship set off for the Knock Deep and sailed around the Ross Revenge in salutation of the oldest offshore station.

Engineer Mike Barrington noticed the Ross Revenge had riggers up in her mast, so switched the `Communicator's transmitters off while they were close so as not to risk giving any of them a shock. He was a little disappointed at their reception: "Peter Chicago had apparently told all the crew on the Ross Revenge not to wave to us as he felt the re-appearance of Laser would be bad news for Radio Caroline," said Mike Barrington. "We waved to them anyway and then sailed off to a new anchorage just a little to the south of Caroline once again."

Just after Laser Hot Hits came back on the air John Anthony remarked that he could only see miserable faces on the Radio Caroline crew as they passed by. He gave out Radio Caroline's address and urged the Laser Hot Hits listeners to write to the Caroline crew and cheer them up.

Interference from a German station was a problem after dark, and the two German stations then using 576 kHz were swamping Laser's signal. The closest was a 250 transmitter at Wobbelin near Schwerin. The interference was a big problem, especially while the ship was transmitting with low power. It was not so bad when she could use around 21 kilowatts and in daylight, but in December around the North Sea there isn't much of that!

Reception was however acceptable over a wide area of eastern England, although nowhere near as good as it had been on the much clearer frequency, 558 kHz. That frequency had been seized by Radio Caroline, the day after Laser had closed, just over a year before.

Newsreader **Andrew Turner** was pressed into service to host some programmes. His was a very well known voice and he had previously been heard on BBC Radio One's daily 'Newsbeat' programmes. Andrew had a solid journalistic grounding in both BBC and commercial radio in the UK. After Laser Hot Hits was silenced, Andrew worked at Blue Danube Radio in Vienna for a while. He then joined LBC in London before moving to *Long Wave Atlantic 252*, Radio Luxembourg's answer to Laser.

A few days after launch another American voice was heard, that of **Paul Dean,** one of Laser 558's original 1984 line up. This was to be Paul's THIRD spell on an offshore radio station, the first two having been Radio North Sea International and Laser 558.

Paul's wasn't the only Laer 558 voice heard; Dave Lee Stone could be heard too, usually presenting a Motown Magic programme, however this was a pre-recorded show that Ray Anderson had found in the ship's archives. It was to come in very useful whenever the complement of DJs was diminished.

A new American DJ heard in the second week on the air for Laser Hot Hits was **KC,** a 28 year old DJ from San Francisco who had many years American radio experience. KC's full name was Kirk Clyatt, and he had been recruited from a station in Las Vegas. It was his first time in the UK and he found the English pubs and trains a novelty, but was not impressed by the B&B accommodation that Laser Hot Hits used in Walton on the Naze, nor the cabins on board. He was prone to seasickness and reported that the food was very limited, "simply pork, beans, potatoes and UHT milk". Luckily he was on the ship at the same time as Paul Dean, who was an excellent cook as well as DJ.

At this time the ship had four or five engineers on board as well as sailors and the station's enigmatic owner, known to most as 'Hughie' who persevered even though his stomach didn't enjoy the sea. Often no one came near the ship for several days and then suddenly they would get a couple of tenders in one day – usually the Lady Gwen from the UK and the Bellatrix from France.

The Bellatrix was a fine Dutch built short sea patrol craft that had been originally fitted with a 3-inch gun and a par of machine guns. Slightly older than the Communicator she had previously been used as a pilot cutter, so was spacious and comfortable. She later changed her name to the ORCA and moved to Lisbon with the Communicator in 1989.

In contrast to the launch of Laser 558, the first few week's shows were well loaded with commercials. Many were small businesses and mail order operations, mostly connected with the music business, but there were big well-known advertisers too. Laser HotHits merchandise was heavily promoted too, with such products as HotHits jigsaw puzzles, a relaunched Communicator Club, and the usual range of full colour posters of the ship.

Listeners could also buy a cassette of Laser jingles (£4) Laser Lover badges with the K "I want to communicate with you" flag in yellow and blue, as well as the inevitable T-shirts or sweat shirts, though the price had now escalated to £12 each.

As well as writing to the usual address on Madison Avenue in New York, listeners were able to order merchandise via a London number. (Laser T shirts and jingles are once again available to buy, along with other Laser merchandise. See http://*worldofradio.co.uk*/*Laser.html*)

Record plugging was very evident and the station's 'PowerPlay' the first week was for Samantha Fox's new release, *I'm all you Want*. As a result, the Radio Authority instructed ILR stations to ban the number and it also received no airplay on the BBC, resulting in only a poor showing in the nether regions of the chart for poor Sam. Sam's previous releases did well, as did her subsequent ones. New programmes included 'Garage Goodies', a daily shop window for new independent artists, who could get their new record on the air for just £65.

As soon as the Communicator recommenced transmissions, the DTI issued a statement saying they would "renew their pursuit of the station with all the vigour they could muster and they were sure that this would have the same result as previously." Despite the reappearance of the Communicator in the Knock Deep, the DTI and its spy boat never reappeared and no overt surveillance was undertaken, other than intermittent fly-pasts by aircraft taking pictures. The two radio ships operated quite overtly, untroubled by the authorities, with tenders operating from several UK ports, not to mention the larger fuel and water runs from Dunkerque.

Peter Baldwin, the Director General of the IBA (Independent Broadcasting Authority, which regulated commercial radio and television) said he had already complained to the Government as their Department of Trade had failed.

On the 4th December the ship's position was given as simply "in the Southern North Sea", while she was in fact just east of the Galloper light float. The following day her exact position was given out during Laser Hot Hits programmes, said to be as a navigational aid to passing ships. The position given was:
51 degrees 42 minutes 32 seconds North,
1 degree   35 minutes 35 seconds East.

Radio Waves International, the Dallas based advertising agency selling the station's airtime operated from an address in Irvine, Texas. RWI announced in December that one of its vice presidents was Robbie Day, who had worked hard to sell time on Laser 558 and who also starred on the Laser Road shows. Despite his very high profile, with appearances at the Laser Road Shows which were advertised in the press all over the country, Robbie was never arrested nor apparently even questioned about his work for Laser.

Only two weeks into its life, Laser HotHits was beset by generator problems. No sooner was that problem solved than the station announced it would have to go off the air due to an arcing insulator at the top of the mast. It could not be fixed in the rough weather, which continued for another eleven days, keeping the station silent. It could not have happened at a worse time, being so soon after launch and in the key month for radio advertising sales, December. Worse was to come: the main aerial array came loose and ended up entangling itself around the masts.

Every cloud has a silver lining and the eleven days down time had given the station a chance to give everyone a short break for Christmas, as the team had worked incredibly hard for the station launch.

When Laser Hot Hits returned to the air on Boxing Day it was not possible to get the full team of DJs back on board again so quickly, and programmes were mainly non stop music and pre-recorded programmes. The weather at this time was still pretty horrendous, and the Communicator had to run its main engines and steam 'half ahead' to take the strain off the anchor chain.

On New Years Eve the station closed suddenly without any announcement. The station's owners had decided that the previous flimsy antenna of lattice masts was not robust enough to survive at sea and they planned replacing them as soon as possible with the solid masts.

On 5th January 1987 Mother Nature stepped in to help the decision along. Gale force winds and a blizzard tore the aerial cables down. "An hour later the front mast split from its base and literally walked along the deck before collapsing," remembers Mike Barrington. Fortunately the ship was manned by several experienced engineers and sailors. "I was in the production studio when the lights died and the ship suddenly rolled really hard," remembers Mike Barrington. "Her nose dived right under and the back end of the ship went way up the in air. I really thought she wasn't going to come back up. Scary!" The thin walled lattice masts buckled under the stress of the many different forces which a ship and anything on it endures in a wild sea. Fortunately, no one was hurt as many of the crew were stranded ashore, celebrating the New Year.

An experienced mast climber, Dennis Jason, had been warning for some weeks that the rigging and masts needed urgent attention. "We really should have done the mast work while we were in Harwich, some work but there was either never any money, or it was a bad time because the DTI were watching the ship."

"As soon as high power was applied when we went back on the air, the aerial started flashing over but no reduction in power was ever made."

The owner's rush to get the ship out to sea and on the air gave the weather chance to wreak more havoc before any remedial action could be taken. The Communicator was now dismasted and silent.

Mast riggers with nothing to climb
Johnny, Mike and Joost on deck
by Dennis Jason

by Paul Alexander Rusling

The array of cables which formed the aerial were normally hung on porcelain insulators. These need to be quite long because the voltages found on aerials that are electrically short (and the aerial on the Communicator was only about 11% of its 514 metres wavelength) considerably less than half of what it ought to have been. This makes problems with a parameter called the 'Q' of an aerial, which was high and that led to fierce voltages on the aerial itself.

The aerials had not been properly secured before the Communicator had left Harwich and it was now impossible to send anyone aloft to renew the insulators. The winter gales were relentless and tore the antenna cables away, one by one.

The ship was now being serviced by the Bellatrix, a Honduran registered vessel that could carry fuel and water. It was often impossible to get a tender alongside the ship due to the high seas running down the Knock Deep channel at the time. Low on fuel, shorn of her aerials and now dismasted; things were not looking good for the Communicator and she faced 1987 with some uncertainty.

Most of those involved in marketing station's airtime from offices in London and New York were former Laser 558 people, led by John Catlett. They included John Cole and Paul Fairs who also ran the Laser Lovers Road Show in the guise of his alter ego, Rob Day. They now faced an even more difficult time selling 'dead air'. Due to the temporary nature of the Communicator's aerial coverage was reduced and the prices of commercials had been cut by half. Even with this huge discount many advertisers refused to pay their bills, as they had often found the station not on the air when they tuned in.

View from the top of the remains of the Communicator's aft mast, showing the insulators for the aerial and the Bellatrix alongside.

By Dennis Jason

At this time Paul Rusling was working for an American, George Otis, on expanding his High Adventure radio network. This is a Christian evangelical organisation at that time operating stations in Lebanon (broadcasting Christian messages into Israel on high power MW and SW transmitters) and in California. High Adventure still operates radio stations in various parts of the world using short wave transmitters to spread the gospel to South America, the Middle East and Africa. George had been offered a licence to broadcast in Asia and wanted the station on the air as soon as possible. It was agreed that a highly mobile installation such as a radio ship was the ideal solution.

Rusling proposed that *High Adventure Ministries* should buy the Communicator which was now idly lying at anchor in the Knock Deep, silenced after its most recent dismasting. Rusling had approached owner Ray over Christmas but a deal wasn't possible; suddenly Ray was now back on the phone, very worried as he now realised it took a lot of cash to keep a radio ship at sea and all the balls (and a signal) in the air. Rusling quickly arranged to take a Panamanian Surveyor out to the ship in January to affirm her seaworthiness. They arrived two days after the big storm, and she looked a sorry sight, with her lattice masts twisted and distorted and no aerial hanging between them. The ship's crew had been forced to chop it free with axes!

The Panamanian surveyor took around two hours to inspect the ship's machinery and to make ultrasound tests on her hull, while Rusling caught up with the incredible news from the engineers and marine crew. He and Mike Barrington spent some time discussing the CSI transmitters and the various generators. On the way back to England, the visitors spoke to a shipyard in Spain and made some tentative arrangements for her to go there and a new antenna to be installed.

The ensuing negotiations with Ray lasted several days he soon realised the extent of the buyer's existing operations and the amount of funds available. Sensing a 'nice little earner' the ship's owner suddenly increased the asking price of the ship, from £125,000 to half a million! The evangelists however were no fools and would not play that sort of game,

George Otis had flown across from California in his private jet, but he wasn't going to be duped out of that much money for a ship, no matter how ideal she was for the job. He withdrew the offer for the Communicator and instructed Rusling to find another vessel for the *Voice of Hope* broadcasts to south east Asia.

The only other 'ready to go' vessel in Europe was the former *Radio Paradijs* ship that had lain under arrest in Amsterdam for five years. George Otis, Paul Rusling and an entourage of shipping experts, flew immediately to Schiphol, visited the ship and made a TV programme on the deck of the ship. Ben Bode, the representative of Radio Paradijs however could not be found and so that deal fell apart. Subsequently, a suitable base was licensed on shore and the site is still on the air today with its transmissions reaching well into China.

**Illustration of the proposed Voice of Hope ship for Asia,
with an HF Yagi on deck and an AM antenna held by a balloon.**

Laser HotHits' owner in Essex told the crew on board the Communicator to make further temporary repairs to the lattice section masts. The proposed 'new' masts would need help from a crane ship to even lift them off the deck, so using two sections of mast stored in the ship's hold and some salvaged sections from the front mast, the rear mast was built up to just over sixty feet.

A new "T-aerial array" was slung between the new rear mast and front ship's mast, thanks to help from Dennis Jason from Surrey, another former Radio Caroline DJ and experienced climber. This got Laser Hot Hits back on the air by the end of January, but only at moderate power and somewhat intermittently.

Two new DJs were heard when the station returned to the air in late January, **DL Bogart** and **Brandy Lee**. They appeared to be the only disc jockeys on the ship, as several of the ship's engineers appeared on the air from time to time to make announcements and request reception reports. Most of them were well known voices previously heard on Radio Caroline.

When the antenna repairs were (temporarilly) completed, full programmes could resume once again. New DJ Brandy Lee was usually heard driving the station's Breakfast Show, with Andrew Turner once again reading news bulletins. Brandy began using a new station slogan, "Never more than a minute away from a seasick bucket," after she had to spend several days in her bunk recovering for the motion of the sea.

Most of the DJs from the original line up, such as Jim Perry and Bill Reid appeared to have not returned to the ship after their Christmas break; even the most enthusiastic voice of all, Johnny Rock'n'Roll Anthony appeared to be on extended shore leave.

On the first of February the station announced that Laser HotHits would be relaunched at 6am the following day and appeared to be running high power once again. Laser Hot Hits reopened with many promotions for its own station merchandise, but they also had commercials for the Sunday Sport newspaper, holiday and some music business products.

DL Bogart made some amazing 'off the cuff' live reads for the Sunday Sport and constantly talked up the feast of heavenly bodies to be found in its pages! He was of course referring to the Sunday Sport's coverage of young ladies, flaunting their mammaries, but he got a bit enthusiastic and likened them to a newspaper like the National Geographic magazine. "The Sunday Sport makes it possible to do some star gazing without having an expensive telescope and without going outside and freezing your bollocks off," explained DL to the Laser Hot Hits listeners. He later apologised for using the mild expletive word on the air.

The new but temporary aerial gave more problems throughout February with only DL Bogart and Brandy Lee on duty most of the time. Often the station spent so few hours on the air each day they could cope. Their programmes were invariably professionally presented and they built up an avid and enthusiastic audience.

At the end of February they were joined by **Paul Jackson**, a DJ from North Carolina, and a new newsreader in the form of **John Allen**. The Communicator now had a crew of nine, including Brandy Lee as the sole lady and the station was again picking up new commercials. Several days were lost in March due to weather, which troubled the aerial, still hanging perilously between the remains of the two lattice masts. Only frequent climbing by Dennis Jason and James Day kept the station on the air. Quite often the seas were so heavy that the engine had to be run for several days to take the strain off the anchor chain as it was now giving some concern.

Dismasted and silent in 1987.

New **DJ Bill Reid** was only heard on Laser Hot Hits for just over a week in March when further problems with the antenna put the station off the air once again. He had previously been heard on KCMU-FM and KJET-AM in Seattle, Washington. He hosted an afternoon show at KNDD, 'The End' for nine years and worked in ComProd at K-Rock. After his trip out to the ship he returned to Seattle where he now runs his own production company.

After midnight, when most of the crew and team were in bed, it could look a bit spooky in some parts of the Communicator. Dennis Jason was working on the transmitter in the early hours of one morning, concentrating very hard on the manual, when he was aware of someone walking towards him. "He was dressed in a red jacket, jeans and black shoes, and greasy hair," he still remembers quite vividly. "I took no notice at first, but instead of continuing into the generator hold, they suddenly went behind the transmitter. I had the PA doors open and went to warn whoever it was, but they had simply disappeared!"

"I didn't think much of it at first. A while later I went up to the bridge to ask if there had been a tender that day while I was asleep and asked who the new guy was. I was amazed when the Captain told me that there had not been a tender and that we had not got any new crew or visitors on board!"

Dennis Jason, where he saw the ghost

"We later found out that, back in 1976, the Gardline days, a young sailor was killed on board in the hold and it's been said by many crewmen that his ghost still walks the decks at night, trying to find another way off." There was a cargo door for the cattle there once but it was welded up during the conversion work in Port Everglades.

The supplies situation on board the Communicator was becoming ever more desperate and the team was sorely depleted. For much of April 1987 the station was run by just three dis jcokeys: Paul Jackson, DL Bogart, and Brandy Lee. Fuel was still a problem and ovber the Easter weekend, DL Bogartannounced "Laser HotHits would like to continue but we're unable to do so without further supplies of diesel." Thames TV and a Sunday newspaper each reported that staff had left the ship due to lack of supplies and had not been paid their wages.

Just after Easter a Laser HotHits spokesman conceded "Technical problems and weather off the coast had meant that we have been unable to pay all the wages for the last month, and the ship is low on fuel which is the major reason for the station being off the air at the moment." He put a brave face on the situation however and claimed that new investors were ready to back Laser and dismissed the wild reports of a mutiny. He also said they would be back in about a week or ten days and added, "all in all the future looks bright."

At the end of April, Laser 558 was once again transmitting only a low power signal due to the critical shortage of fuel. The ship was also low on fresh water and food, with the crew worried that the ship could be snatched at any moment by creditors. The ship left the air on 26th April and ten days later went into Harwich, where an emergency crew was placed on board.

In May the ship moved to a new anchorage not far off Felixstowe so that more materials could be delivered to rebuild the antenna system. The two lighting stanchions had found their way out to the ship, but needed a crane to erect them.

In May 1987, Ray Anderson of EAP flew to New Jersey where he met with Paul Rusling, who was by now engaged on yet another new radio project. Paul introduced Ray to James Ryan, who just three years previously had brokered the multi-million dollar deal to fund Radio Caroline and the purchase of the Ross Revenge radio ship.

Paul Rusling and Ray Anderson at James Ryan's NJ home

After a period of illness Ryan was now living with his young wife Ursula and their two daughters on a ranch in Egg Harbor, New Jersey. It's a short drive from Atlantic City, where the Summer saw some very interesting meetings. Funding was available from a shipping magnate from Norway who had his own shipyard and three oil tankers. A bulk carrier had been bought in Nova Scotia to be converted with a huge budget of millions of dollars, but this would all take some time.

Along with Viacom, the new group were planning to enter the television merket in Europe and a floating radio station was thought to be an ideal promotional vehicle, if the ship could be readied quickly and be on the air before November. Ray Anderson assured James Ryan that "The Communicator is in great condition and nearly ready to switch on again, although will need a little work on the aerial." In fact what it needed was the aerial system erecting, not an easy job out at sea!

James Ryan made Ray Anderson a good offer for his interest in the Communicator and effectively bought him out at that time. Given Ray's lack of business experience and desperation to get funding for the ship, which was costing him every penny he had to keep out at sea, the wily American was easily able to persuade him to accept his first offer. The deal included taking over the supply runs and paying off the debts that had accrued.

The transaction however was paid for with paper in a quoted company that Ryan had founded called the *Walker Corporation*. Ray impressed on the new owner the importance of getting supplies out to the ship and Ryan promised to attend to this immediately.

Fuel and water for the ship had been supplied from Dunkerque by the Honduras flagged ships, the MV Bellatrix and the MV Windy, which had been named after the owner, Fred Bolland's dog. A large amount was owed for supplies from the first few months of 1987 and Fred was a bit concerned the bills would go unpaid, now that the ship had new owners. After getting more information on the situation, Fred decided to take control of the radio ship to take care of it.

They moved the Communicator to a new mooring near the Fairy Bank, fifteen miles north of Dunkerque, with the assistance of the Bellatrix. This new location made it much easier to supply the ship and to keep a close watch over it and any movements.

Fred Bolland's pride and joy – MV Bellatrix.

Within days Fred Bolland had a phone call from a lawyer from Atlantic City who said he was acting for James Ryan who represented the ship's new owners. "Ryan's lawyer asked me to come to the United States to resolve the case," said Fred. "I told him that I was prepared to come to the USA after the bill was settled and the next day the bill was paid in full!" Ryan was by now involved in several other projects including one called *Radio Ursula*, named after his wife, but none of these ever began broadcasting. They seemed to be schemes to simply raise money from investors using the promise of the fun and excitement of radio and nebulous promises of "treasure at the end of the rainbow."

By mid August the Communicator was on the move again, this time to a mooring about fifteen miles from Felixstowe, in the Galloper channel, to make it easier for backers for another new station to see the ship. These new backers had been introduced by Paul Fairs, who was living near Ipswich, the closest city to Felixstowe from where the ship could now be seen. Two local tug firms and even some local pilots were kept busy ferrying Laser personnel and proepective buyers out to the ship.

The crew on board the Communicator by this time was pretty minimal in order to keep costs down. The owner was still 'financially embarrassed'. At one stage DJ Paul Jackson sailed the ship single-handed to a new mooring, about ten miles away. P`aul was a very capable and useful person to have on board a radio ship; he later worked in law enforcement. Paul is seen here on the right with Captain Bob who served on the Communicator for a time.

Among the prospective buyers of the ship were a British evangelist called Stephen Morgan, who was keen to operate his own religious station from the ship, to be called **Harmony Radio 981**. He had previously had his programmes aired on Caroline's Viewpoint service.

A wealthy man with extensive property interests Stephen lived in some opulence in south London and had another home in Kent. He handed over almost six figures to Laser executives but very little of it reached the ship in the form of parts or supplies and he never saw any return for his investment.

The pop service previously operating as *Laser HotHits* would also return. It was planned to broadcast its usual format of hits and in order to have a fresh start, and shake off some creditors, the station would be renamed **Starforce 576**. Laser's advertising team claimed that many of the best known Laser DJs would be returning to the station and they kept on running the Laser Lovers road show while waiting for the Communicator to be upgraded with a new aerial system

14. RADIO SUNK

Further repair work was done to the Communicator; the old masts were taken down in September in a ploy to convince the authorities the ship was not about to resume broadcasting. The Communicator was reminded what really heavy seas were like again in October when even by running her engine continuously, she could not remain on station and dragged her anchor for about twenty miles before finding calmer waters. By the end of October 1987 the MV Communicator was anchored just a few miles from the Sunk light vessel. Johnny Lewis was still working on board and, to keep the transmitters dry and the damp at bay, he ran them for an hour every day.

After a while, Johnny got a little bit bored doing nothing, so decided to make some programmes and launch his own radio station. The crew had just taken down the remaining sections of lattice masts and not yet found a way to put up the more solid 'lamp post' style masts, which were sat on the deck.

Johnny 'broadcast' his Radio Sunk programmes using the dummy load. This is a large resistive component that allows the transmitters to be tested into as an alternative to an antenna, without radiating very much signal. Unfortunately Radio Sunk caused some damage to an RF choke in the final remaining transmitter; a simple copper coil it just exploded and would have cost around £200 to replace from the manufacturers.

The only listeners able to hear these leaked transmissions would have been the five man crew of the Trinity House light ship nearby and a few passing vessels. Radio Sunk was very short lived and 'very restricted coverage' but recordings exist. It was probably the least heard of all the ship's transmissions!

The Sunk name came from a nearby lightship which has now been replaced by an unmanned LANBY (light & navigational buoy). The 'Sunk' area is well known as a 'radio calling in point' for shipping approaching the Thames Estuary's ports and it marks the start of an important shipping separation zone just off Felixstowe, east of Sealand.

Ten days later the Communicator moved back to her previous anchorage in the Knock Deep where a spokesman told journalists that the new owners of the ship were well versed in broadcasting without breaking the Marine Offences Act. "We are more than sufficiently funded to relaunch two radio stations from the ship and hope to be broadcasting again very soon," he said.

An uneventful Christmas and New Year was spent by the Communicator in her usual anchorage in the Knock Deep but with only a skeleton crew on board. Legal problems over transfer of ownership of the vessel were still lumbering on, with James Ryan still trying to persuade Ray Anderson to sign more papers to enable him to release further funds.

A full schedule of debts outstanding in the name of the ship was sent to Ryan's lawyer Don Phillips in Atlantic City on Christmas Eve 1987, which everyone hoped would now lead to some progress being made and more money pumped into the project so that the work on raising the antennas and restarting broadcast could be made.

There was more trouble and drama in the small hours of the 12th of January 1988 when the skeleton crew woke to find themselves the subject of another attempted takeover. Three security guards were immediately hired to care for the ship, but just a few days later the raiders were back once again with three boats of heavies. They claimed that they were there to protect the assets of one of the backers of the new station, but wouldn't give any names or clues to the identity of the owners.

Fiona Jeffreys with stalwart engineer Mike Barrington
by Chris Edwards

Less than three weeks later, on the 3rd February, the ship lost her last anchor and had to steam back into Harwich where she tied up alongside Parkestone Quay once again. The ship's crew told inspectors from the Department of Trade that the owners had decided to take the radio equipment off and sell the ship for scrap, which helped to keep the authorities off their back for a while.

The radio ship was moved across the River Stour from Parkestone Pier to the familiar anchorage off Erwarton, where a High Court writ was served on behalf of local suppliers *Harwich Marine Services* a few days later, despite engineer Mike Barrington's assurances that he had their money ashore. Inspectors from the DTI went on board and disabled the two transmitters by removing key components.

Mike spent almost a year living on board the Communicator at this time, in addition to his regular duties of security out on Sealand. A very capable engineer and seaman, he had his first radio dalliances with Radio Jackie, a station in London. Mike, American DJ Paul Jackson and Dennis Jason joined the Communicator's ghost keeping watch over the ship for the next twelve months.

On 6th February the Communicator was moved across the River Stour and beached 'bows on' to the mud banks at the scrapyard at Mistley, two miles further up the Stour, near Manningtree. An enterprising farmer charged visiting enthusiasts one pound each to cross his land and see the ship. At low tide the ship was 'high and dry' on the mud.

A lot of the studio kit was removed from the ship during her 1988 stay at Mistley, not to mention most of the bridge fittings. With the DTI having disabled the transmitters by clipping some connections and most of the studio kit removed, she seemed to have been almost forgotten by her owner. The ship's caretakers had little to do and were each guarding her for different bosses, as the ownership battles over the vessel were still dragging on.

The MV Communicator at Mistley scrap yard
Note the original masts along the starboard side

by Paul Alexander Rusling

ANALYSIS OF LASER HOT HITS' PROBLEMS

So what had gone wrong with the latest attempt to launch Laser from the Communicator? Once access could be had to the financial records, such as they were, of the Laser Hot Hits project, comparisons could be made to the Laser 558 escapade. The Hot Hits incarnation should have been a huge financial success for several reasons. Firstly, it had much lower operating costs than the original Laser 558. Secondly, the huge cost of converting the ship, buying and installing the transmitters and other equipment had all been paid, indeed even the bare bones purchase of the ship came in at a heavily discounted price. East Anglian Productions had paid a fraction of what the ship had cost initially.

Laser Hot Hits had also avoided paying huge marketing costs run up by Roy Lindau in the station's first year, when just over £550,000 had been spent running the New York office with precious little to show for it, other than managing to antagonise key people who just might have been able to make it work. Some executives did rather well out of the Laser 558 escapade with the top three executives each pocketing amounts well into six figures.

Many of the Communicator crew and DJs worked for up to 11 weeks on board for just a few hundred pounds for their hard work and sacrifices. Some left the project owed money or had to fight through the courts to get the money they had paid out.

Laser Hot Hits had the benefit of a great brand name and an experienced team. While the new station did have some of the old baggage who had muddled around at Laser 558, they had a good team of DJs, some first class engineers and competent advertising salesmen, who were able to bring in some income. What they were short of was enough capital to complete the job, to make sure the aerial was sufficiently robust to ride out winter storms. They also failed to ensure that the Communicator was sufficiently well stocked, and supply tenders sorted, with enough food, oil and water to operate for at least six months.

The usual killer for many businesses had struck again; the project was simply under-capitalised. Such a shame for a project that should have been able to turn over £5m a year. The UK had no national commercial radio stations and most of the well-run local stations managed well over a million a year turnover with much smaller audiences. Radio Luxembourg was grossing over £9m a year from its night time only service in English, although they had huge energy costs to feed their 1.3 million watt transmitter!

Early in 1989, discussions took place with more prospective buyers, including some of the operators of *Cable One*, a Dutch station that broadcast from London by satellite. They proposed a new station called Radio Europa which they intended to operate legally, supplied from Spain. The project included many former Radio Veronica DJs and a well-known Dutch record promoter, with over 1.5 million Guilders of backing.

In early April 1989 the ship left Harwich for the final time, with Fred Bolland at the helm. The *Cord Cabo* company had now been been bought by Fred's *Waipuna Anstalt*, a Liechtenstein registered foundation.

While in Harwich the ship had been stripped of most equipment, although the transmitters remained, but she needed new navaids & SOLAS kit. Waipuna hired a British tug to tow the ship from Harwich to Lisbon in Portugal where work to refurbish her was to be carried out, but it broke down off Dover.

Captain Fred Bolland
(by Leendert Vingerling)

The Communicator was moored by the Fairy Bank bank off Dunkerque where she remained until the end of June. There she had replacement anchors fitted and was filled with fuel and water. Radio engineer José van Groningen did work while there on the ship's transmitters, the two CSI MW units for two different frequencies and a powerful short wave unit. There was also a 30kW FM transmitter from *Radio Paradijs* to be used to reach Belgium. The Paradijs *Optimod* processor was also delivered to the ship while off Dunkerque.

New anodes and port of registry
By Fred Bolland

By July she was in Lisbon and work continued to bring her back 'into class'. While in dry dock other work was also done; some areas of her hull were replated and new anodes fitted as well as a fresh coat of deep green paint and her new port of registry, San Lorenzo. A new client wanted to broadcast right wing fundamental Christianity to Romania. This was the 'Underground Church' based in the USA, Germany and Holland, who were paying one and a half million Guilders via the *White Lanca Marine* of Panama for airtime on the ship.

Two German agents whose history included paramilitary activities and recruiting mercenaries were representing the Underground Church. Their involvement so concerned the Dutch secret service that they decided to act against the two radio ships. On the 20th of August, agents of the Buitenlandse Veiligheidsdienst (BVD) staged an illegal raid on the Caroline ship, the Ross Revenge during which armed thugs forcibly closed all three of the ship's transmitters: *Radio Caroline*, *Radio Monique* and *World Mission Radio*.

WMR was of greatest concern as it could be heard all over Europe but no one knew what its purpose was. The agents convictions for recruiting merceneraries were a good excuse; they were said to be dangerous to the Netherlands' delicate political make up. 'Protecting the Dutch state' was their excuse. The raiders took most of the equipment and both the Dutch and religious services were never heard again but Radio Caroline broadcasts resumed just six weeks later.

The Communicator's new masts were replaced and more ballast was added plus three new Mitsubishi generators. Former Radio Veronica engineer José van Groningen and Fred Bolland worked hard on the transmitters, especially the Short Wave which would be the main 'money spinner'. She now looked superb in her gleaming green coat of paint

A smart new coat of green paint for the Communicator in Lisbon

The British and Dutch authorities urged their Portuguese counterparts to act against the Communicator claiming its capability to transmit four different radio stations, including short wave, was "dangerous to international relations." The Portuguese were told that the German agents were "conspiring to act against Holland'. As a result she was raided while in Lisbon and a lot of the radio equipment removed.

This initiative also brought about a harsh new clause in the UK's new Broadcasting Act a few months later, extending jurisdiction over parts of the high seas, although the clause has not yet been tested. The clause was inserted during a House of Lords reading with members told that it was required for reasons of national security to secure passage. It was not debated in the House of Commons and the new measure extends powers to officials enabling them to board foreign ships beyond British waters if unlicensed broadcasts are suspected.

The downfall of Romania's leader, Nicolae Caucescu, made the Romanian project unnecessary and the funding from the Underground Church company, *White Lanca*, dried up. The Communicator was temporarily renamed the MV Albatross in June 1993 and sold to the *Old Court Shipping Company* of Panama City, who changed her name back again after just three months.

**Alongside in Lisbon in 1992
(an unused mast configuration)**

Over the following winter she was visited by two prospective buyers and eventually a deal was struck for her to re-enter the world of radio, as a fully licensed radio station.

Instead of been moored out at sea, at the mercy of the wind and waves in the mouth of the Thames Estuary, she would now be securely tied up alongside, on an inland Dutch waterway.

The long promised and eagerly awaited riches for the Communicator were fginally about to materialise. Just over the horizon were contracts to transmit radio stations that would bring in large amounts of advertising revenue.

Part 2
Inland in the Netherlands

15. DUTCH PRIVATES BECOME LEGAL

Meanwhile in the Netherlands, the Dutch Government had been considering how it might permit private radio stations to broadcast. Stations had successfully broadcast programmes via London registered satellite outlets which were relayed on cable networks throughout the Netherlands, a country where over 90% of homes had access to cable TV.

The leading station was Cable One, a cooperative of many former Radio Caroline, Monique and Veronica DJs, which was partly funded by Rupert Murdoch's News International. As part of the introduction of regular private radio stations, a few selected broadcasters were permitted to transmit for an experimental period while a system of licensing was devised.

Among these were Sky Radio and a sister station, Sky HitRadio which in 1992 became Radio 538. These stations were run from the former TV studios at the Concordia cinema in Bussum by Radio Veronica DJ Lex Harding and the last Dutchman on the Radio Caroline ship before it sank, Ton Lathouwers. Another successful 'experimental' station was Happy RTL. This was financed by Radio Luxembourg's owners CLT and run by another former Radio Caroline DJ, Ruud Hendriks, also known as Rob Hudson.

Eventually, in 1983 the Dutch Government advertised for bids to operate a new tier of private radio stations. On offer were three networks of AM frequencies and two networks of FM frequencies, each offering near national coverage. 27 groups submitted bids, however there could only be five winners. The losers included giants Sky Radio, Happy RTL and many more Dutch media giants, which many assumed would get licences.

The biggest surprise was Radio 538, which only later was given some regional frequencies. A few years later, in 2003, Radio 538 bought a national network of frequencies around 102 FM, but had to pay €57 million for it.

Sky Radio fought a difficult court case against the Ministry to win a high power frequency allocation, 100.5 FM, which had been used by local Radio

Utrecht at low power. (Former Communicator engineer Paul Rusling played a role in this too, but the Sky Radio story is complex and outside the scope of this book).

They were even more surprised, and a little perplexed, with a foreign bid called Classic *f*M assembled by Paul Rusling, that was accepted and awarded one of the two national FM networks. The promised format was a curious mixture of jazz and classical music which he felt would appeal to the two Ministers awarding the licences. The other FM network was awarded to RNN – Radio Noordzee Nationaal, whose funders had operated from a ship moored off Scheveningen in the early 1970s. RNN proposed playing mostly Dutch language music and undertook not try to compete with the pop music service, Hilversum III.

Three further 'packets' of unused AM frequencies were also awarded:

A. 1395 kHz **Elle Magazine**

B. 675 kHz **Radio 10 Gold**

C. 1224 & 828 kHz **Holland FM**

The first frequency, on 1395 kHz was licensed for use with 500kW of power which would have given huge coverage had it not been for an unlicensed station that used the same frequency after dark. The competitor was a relay transmitter for *Trans World Radio*, in Albania to blast a signal after dark to Germany. Whoever wanted to use 1395 in Holland would have to tolerate that intrusion, three hours of German religious broadcasts each evening.

The publishers of Elle Magazine were awarded the 1395 slot and planned a mainly speech based station. After a lot of expensive consulting and heart-searching, they concluded that the incoming interference wrought by the TWR transmitter in Albania after dark could render their station unprofitable. Two locations planned for the 1395 transmitter, either at Flevopolder, where NOZEMA already operated a pair of masts on 747 and 1008 kHz. The existing two signals were of 400 kilowatts and 200 kilowatts and would have coped with the 1395 output quite easily, with some additional aerial tuning and matching equipment. The cost however would be charged to the account of the new user of the frequency. Given that only a five-year licence had been issued, the owners of Elle believed that the cost was too expensive, so they handed back their licence.

Packet B was for a single frequency of 675 kHz that had been used by the Dutch Station Broadcaster, the NOS, in the 1980s for its pop music programme, Hilversum III. It used a single transmitter facility at Lopik, just south of Utrecht to achieve national coverage. Since Hilversum III moved to an FM network, the Dutch state transmission organisation, NOZEMA, had broadcast a simple hiolding announcement at low power.

Radio 10 Gold's award of the 675 frequency also took the licensee by surprise. Radio 10 was run by yet another former Radio Caroline DJ, Jeroen Soer, which evolved from the *Cable One* station that had originally transmitted from London, at least on paper. Jeroen decided very quickly that if he must have his station on AM it must have a 'gold' programme format. He moved very quickly, secured a deal for NOZEMA to transmit Radio 10 from the existing Lopik site, changedits output to a Gold format, had a large campaign of advertising contracted and was ready to start broadcasting within two weeks.

There were however a couple of problems with the 675 transmitter at Lopik, but Jeroen Soer, the MD of Radio 10, knew a man who could help. He had already signed a contract with Paul Rusling to install audio processing at the transmitter site. The facility had been redundant for some years pending the award of licenses for private radio. Now only one out of four units was working. Many NOZEMA engineers with experience of AM had now retired and were not available to recommission it.

Rusling was asked by NOZEMA to look at the stubborn 675 AM transmitters. The installation comprised four 30kW Nautel units, only one of which would fire up. After a couple of hours work he had all four running at full power and the Optimod audio processor correctly adjusted, making Radio 10 sound incredibly loud. Testing the 675 installation at Lopik was done by calling up his contacts across Europe, including in the UK, to ask for audio comparison tests. It was soon clear that Radio 10 Gold was now heard as far south as Paris, west to Birmingham, north to Stockholm and eastwards to Berlin.

Paul Rusling making adjustments to Nozema's 675 transmitter at Lopik

For the third AM Network (C in the table above) there were much poorer prospects. There was no transmitter site available for 1224, and for the second frequency, 828, only one site was available, for just one kilowatt. The lucky licensee was Holland FM, who, as their name suggests, had hoped to get an FM network. The company grew out of City FM, StadsRadio in Rotterdam, run by merchant banker Gerro Vonk and Nico Volker, who were also partners in Radio Monique with Fred Bolland.

NOZEMA proposed having a transmitter at the Trintelhaven for 1224. This is a small yachting 'harbour of refuge' half way along the dyke that runs for about 30km between Lelystad and Enkhuizen, along the south western corner of the IJsselmeer. It was sufficiently distant from any habitation so unlikely to be objected to on environmental grounds. Still however there were potentially problems with getting planning permission for a mast, so it was decided that the stations would use a mast on board the Communicator; to transmit from a ship does not need any planning p[ermission as it is not a permanent structure.

Holland FM hurriedly launched on the 828AM channel with just a kilowatt using the single 35M mast at Heinenoord, just a couple of kilometres south of Rotterdam. It was woefully inadequate and suffered from incoming interference from the many other stations that also used 828 kHz in neighbouring countries.

The Communicator underway, with three tugs in attendance.

16. HOLLAND FM

Finding a transmitter site for 1224 kHz, which could give near national coverage, was difficult due to planning restrictions. The Dutch are very sensitive about their environment; they built a lot of their land literally 'by hand' over the last few generations by reclamation and have strict planning laws. Approval for a radio mast could take years, so it was suggested that they operate from a ship, which would be outside the reach of Dutch planning laws. It was a creative but simple way to get the station on the air and an excellent way to generate publicity for a new radio station.

Enter once again the good ship Communicator. She had been laid up in Lisbon for a few years but maintained in good condition. A deal was quickly concluded for $100,000 from a Portuguese company called *Preparacoes Navais do Jego* on the 3rd June 1994. After a little preparation, she left Lisbon within a few weeks and on the 11th August she arrived at IJmuiden, being towed astern by the tug *Vlieland!*

The ship was repainted overall with the colours of the Dutch flag of red, white and blue and he port of registry was now Rotterdam. She looked really bright and clean, almost like the inside of a hospital. In IJmuiden a team of specialists re-installed one of the masts just for'ard of the hatches and erected various regulation safety measures including a two meter high fence and locked gates to prevent people touching live aerial feeds.

Communicator being towed into Ijmuiden harbour, by her stern

Nozema and Harris engineers installed a new Harris DX50 transmitter, the very latest 'all solid state' model. In bright white cabinets, it replaced the two CSI 25 kW units, which were rather unceremoniously shunted into hold space on the tweendeck. They were still in good working order, but had not been run at full power since the 729 tests with the balloons in 1983.

Her new antenna mast was erected on 30th August. It reached 55 metres into the sky and was installed 'alongside' the quay in calm conditions, taking only fifty minutes to secure. Two cranes from Holland's top 'high reach' experts *van Duivenbode* and *van Seumeren* made the job look so easy.

Previous masts on the ship had been erected at sea, without cranes, using only manpower and gin poles. This is why the old masts for Laser 558 and Laser Hot Hits were so lightweight and ultimately why they continually failed. The stress and compression from having a tall structure on a ship are higher and more complex than those found on dry land.

There are six continually changing forces (pitching, heaving, rolling, swaying, surging and yawing) creating unimaginable stress. It's not all brought down into the base of the mast, but some is transmitted through the guy wires (also called stays) and each point of stress must be carefully calculated, a job for specialist naval architects.

The cylindrical mast was grounded at the base, not needing an insulator. Around the mast was hung a cage of vertical wires, offset by about a metre, which formed one half of the aerial, running vertically up the mast. It was connected near the top, a match often known as shunt feeding, with the mast forming the return half down to ground.

The mast was painted alternate red and white bands, although this was not a legal requirement. EU regulations did however demand that a substantial safety barrier be put into place, along with anti-climbing measures to ensure that no one could touch the live cables. These arrangements had to be inspected and approved before NOZEMA's engineers could operate any of the equipment connected to the antenna.

The mast was too heavy to be simply fixed to the top deck of the ship and further reinforcement sections had to be installed in the tween deck and the lower deck to act as a strong foundation and spread the load throughout the ship.

This meant specially forging foundation blocks. The antenna mast required a complex system of guy wires to hold it rigidly in place. These had to be insulated at irregular intervals along their length and then finally tied off with guy anchors.

Those in turn were connected into bespoke guy anchors that had to be affixed to the correct places on the deck of the Communicator. Each location of guy anchors had to be thoroughly tested to ensure it would stand the strain of the mast that required use of the latest state of the art scanning equipment.

The ship was simultaneously fitted with a new Harris DX50 totally solid state 50,000 watt AM transmitter. This was the first marine installation for Harris and they had to hire in engineers with experience of working on ships.

The DX series of transmitters were the latest type, with all solid-state circuitry – not a single valve was used at all. This made very large savings in terms of energy consumption, removed the most fragile components and it made operation possible with much lower voltages. Not so much a problem on land, but at sea on a ship, the dampness means that arcing and other undesirable effects are often found, due to the dampness in the air. Transmitters on land are usually installed with air conditioning plant, to keep the air inside the transmitter cool and to keep it dry. This can be very difficult to achieve on board a ship, so a solid-state transmitter has many advantages.

The DX50 transmitter was installed in the same place that the CSI transmitters had been, on the hatch plates covers leading to the bottom deck (which just contained sand ballast in boxes. It was also right in the path of the ship's ghost, although none of the installation team reported any manifestations. The Harris DX transmitter was invented by Hilmer Swanson at Harris and has since been used to replace many of the Marconi transmitters used for high power in the UK. They can be found with power levels up to 2,000 kilowatts.

The Communicator's Harris DX50 transmitter

The DX transmitters have stacks of transistorised modules of about 1.5 kW each to build up the power to the chosen level. If one of these fails, it simply switches out of circuit, enabling the transmitter to continue functioning, just with that power module lost, i.e. as *n-1* kilowatts output. This avoids the need to have a spare transmitter in standby mode, making for better efficiency and quite a saving in capital cost. The power savings are quite impressive too – a DX50 has typical efficiency of around 93%, much better than many other AM transmitters. The DX on the ship had only one fault in the eight years it ran.

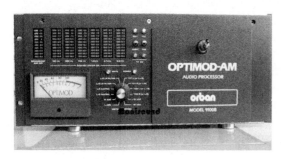

A new 9100B Optimod audio processor was installed in a separate housing in the transmitter room, along with a locked front control plate to prevent any over enthusiastic disc jockeys from tampering with it, to make their own programmes sound even louder.

Two new generators were obtained and installed on the ship, once again with all the safety measures imaginable. The two new generators arrived skid mounted but without anti-vibration mountings which had to be retrofitted.

The two studios at the aft end of the Communicator had been worked on for several weeks. Some areas of soundproofing were repaired and a new coat of paint applied. New mixing desks were installed in both the main on air and the production studio and play out equipment.

Eight weeks later the Communicator was ready to sail to her new mooring at the Trintelhaven, a 'harbour of refuge' for yachts on the Ijsselmeer between Lelystad and Enkhuizen. Within a few hours everything was ready to be switched on and, after a few more aerial tuning adjustments, the Communicator was soon broadcasting with a full 50,000 watts. This was the first time she had broadcast with full power since the balloon aerial tests in January 1984.

The team from Holland FM were impatient to start. They were already facing a problem selling advertising being on the medium wave band, especially in the face of such strong competition as Radio 10 now gave on 675kHz, who began in January.

Holland FM's Programme Director Nico Volker had some top names ready to broadcast on the station: *de gezelligste op de Midden Golf.*

The programmes of Holland FM included many well-known radio presenters, including Eddy Becker, who was something of a national institution throughout the Netherlands. Eddy began his radio career as a newsreader and then as the breakfast DJ on Radio Veronica in the mid 1960s. *Eddy Bekker met de Wekker* (Eddy and the alarm clock) and was a hip, fast talking, up-tempo DJ.

Eddy had been lured from Radio Veronica onto the Dutch state broadcaster, Hilversum III where he became even better known and hosted a TV programme called *Eddy Ready Go.* Eddy had also been a singer on his own (known usually as Eddy Jones) as well as in a couple of groups for a while. Eddy returned to his traditional breakfast slot on Holland FM, where he was heard each weekday morning from 7 to 10am.

40 years a DJ – Eddy Becker

Some years later Eddy launched an excellent magazine called *Flashback* but it almost bankrupted him, so high was the quality. Eddy can still be heard on nostalgia station *Radio 192*.

Others heard following Eddy's morning show were international singing star and actress Ilona Cechova, Frans v/d Drift, Krijn Torringa, Peter de Groot, Jan van Zanten and Chiel Montagne. Weekends on Holland FM saw an even bigger variety of guest presenters with many well-known artists, including Eddie Ouwens, Ad Koppendrayer and world renowned vocalist **Yvonne Keeley.**

Holland FM's superstar Yvonne Keeley

Yvonne began her singing career in London and was the girlfriend of Steve Harley – she can be heard singing on his smash hit *Make Me Smile*. Yvonne also worked with internationally known vocalists Madeline Bell and Vicki Brown before linking up with Scott Fitzgerald for her big UK hit *If I Had Words*, which sold more than a million copies.

Later Yvonne formed The Star Sisters, who had many hits in the 1980s. They were especially glamorous and seen on TV almost daily. They even hit the Top 10 in the UK with their *Stars on 45* medley.

On Holland FM Yvonne hosted a very popular show each week called *Voor de Familie*. She had a great radio voice and was part of a star studded 'De Nationaal Zondag' day on the station each Sunday. Already a popular face on Dutch TV and veteran of many 'sell out' concerts, Yvonne had no problem attracting lots of listeners across the Benelux and northern Germany, where the Holland FM signal would be clearly heard, thanks to the Communicator being sat on one of the biggest inland lakes in Europe, which helps propagate radio signals.

Her colleague **Jan van Zanten** had previously been known as Jan Zwart, broadcasting on several pirate stations on land and at sea. He was known as Sebastian Black on Radio Monique in the mid 80s. In 1992 Jan joined Holland FM where he had more success when he presented *Café De Gulle Lach*.

Jan soon progressed to become one of the most popular DJs heard from the Communicator until 1998 when she stepped up even further to *Veronica fM* and *Yorin FM*, a later radio station in the Veronica group. The station also took some unknown DJs and turned them into superstars; people such as Robert Jensen and Rick Romijn.

The ship was very well cared for at this time by a residential crew who kept it not only secure but in excellent condition. Trintelhaven was a good half an hour drive away from any other human habitation and the Communicator was being managed at this time by Walter Zwart, who had previously worked on Radio Monique, which also broadcast from the Ross Revenge as Walter Simons. He also broadcast on Radio 819, staying for 4½ years.

So strong was the signal at that time on 1224, that Virgin Radio who had just launched on the adjacent channel 1215AM in the UK held several meetings to consider taking over the new outlet, as they were very impressed by its sound, compared to their own transmitter, especially in Eastern England. Holland FM was now widely heard throughout the west and northern parts of the Netherlands. To many people it may have been a mystery why Holland FM continued using the low powered 828AM frequency, especially while it was only really useful in the immediate area around Rotterdam. Many Dutch listeners wondered why Holland FM had such a misleading name when it could only be found on the AM band? Dutch radio is full of such curiosities!

New Years Eve on the Communicator, 1994
Mirjam Verhoof, Walter Zwart, Marjo Marcus,
Leendert Vingerling and Nico Volker celebrating!

17. HOLLAND HITRADIO & HITRADIO 1224

By the New Year the Communicator's 1224 AM transmitter was attracting a large number of listeners. It was decided to change the name; first it became **Holland HitRadio**, replacing the rather misleading 'FM' part of the name with 'HitRadio'. This was a short lived station, because only a few months later, the name 'Holland' was dropped and the AM frequency added, making the name **HitRadio 1224**. This latest new name was used on the air for only a few months, as it was really a precursor to a much bigger change to the radio transmissions from the MV Communicator

Holland FM's homegrown radio star, Jan van Zanten, who was also known as Jan Zwart, felt the urge to adopt a more up to date name. He suddenly became known as Jan Paparazzi! Jan had come a long way from his first steps in radio in the Knock Deep channel, where he broadcast on Radio Monique.

The station was also now more attractive to the really big radio stars and attracted **Edwin Evers** and Gijs Staverman to join them. Edwin began his career on Extra 108 in Amsterdam before getting a job as reserve DJ on Radio 10 Gold. He then joined Power FM and finally assisted Lex Harding with his Veronica programmes on Hilversum III, the Dutch national state pop music station

Edwin's period presenting his 'Evers in the Morning' brought more listeners than the station ever had before, proving that the popularity for the DJ and his personality can be a key component in a radio station's success.

The name 'HitRadio' was not exactly a new one for the Communicator. It had almost been used for a new service from the Communicator in 1988 as part of the *Starforce HitRadio 576* name, however various disputes over funding and problems with the antenna at that time meant it was never used.

The name HitRadio wasn't exactly unknown in the Netherlands; in 1992, Sky Radio were partners in a station with Lex Harding using the HitRadio branding for about six months. In December 1992 the station dropped 'HitRadio' and was renamed Radio 538, in honour of the final medium wavelength used by Radio Veronica during her years at sea.

Once again a top Dutch radio station had a name, that was not only irrelevant to the band it was found on (Radio 538 was always on FM, except in a small corner of the country) but the numbers 538 were to honour a previous radio station,

Veronica, of twenty years before. Dutch Radio is a very curious world but unlike many countries it does have a unique and fascinating character. Radio 538 became eventually the biggest and most listened to radio station in the country, a title they were still holding, and consolidating, in mid 2016.

In the summer, another very well known Dutch radio DJ **Jeroen van Inkel** joined HitRadio 1224. He said he had left the station's top state broadcaster, Hilversum III, simply because he didn't want to work there any more. He now wanted to be where the success was, to have a good fun packed and exciting time on HitRadio 1224.

Jeroen began his career with local stations in the Amsterdam area, before joining Veronica while it was the VOO. There he teamed up with Adam Curry and Rob Stenders, pioneering 'double-header' programmes in the Netherlands. Jeroen also hosted a very popular show on Hilversum III called *Rinkel van Inkel*. He is still on the air, now also writes novels and won the Marconi Oeuvre award.

Gijs Staverman began his radio career on a land pirate station, Radio Galaxy. He also worked on a couple of Amsterdam stations, including Counterpoint FM and some stations in Belgium. In 1991 he joined Veronica to host *Oh What a Night* with Francis Dix and Wessel van Diepen. After hosting the Top 40 show he presented *Staverman op Tilt* and joined HitRadio 1224 in early 1975.

In just a few months, thanks to some good publicity and hiring a team of disc jockeys with an established following, HitRadio1224 attracted a large audience. The station was soon bringing in the equivalent of over six million dollars a year, and the Communicator never lost a single minute of downtime, thanks to the engineering team at NOZEMA.

18. VERONICA HITRADIO

Behind the scenes, Holland FM's new station *HitRadio1224* was in the process of being sold. The buyer was VOO – the Veronica Omroep Organisatie. This was the brainchild of Rob Out, a former Radio Veronica DJ. After Dutch radio ships became illegal under a new law in 1974, the VOO obtained 'public' status in 1975 to allow it to broadcast programmes on the state radio (and TV) networks. A year later they had over a million subscribers for their magazine.

The VOO was better known to most people as Radio Veronica. It was the most popular broadcaster in the Netherlands, having begun on board a ship off the Dutch coast in 1960. Legislation in 1974 meant forced it to leave its anchorage off Scheveningen and join the state broadcasting system. There it had to share its programmes on the three (later four) Dutch stations with about ten mainly political and religious organisations. Veronica now also had to operate as a public foundation and not make any profit.

By 1993 the Dutch parliament had decided to allow commercial private radio and TV in the Netherlands. The key Veronica organisers now wanted to join them and buying an existing licensee was the quickest way to do it. The owners of the FM outlets (*Classic FM* and *Radio Noordzee Nationaal*) had clear programme content commitments written into their licences which clashed with the Veronica ideals, so Holland FM's HitRadio operation were the natural target.

**The Communicator moored at the Bull Verweij pier at Trintelhaven
(named to honour one of the founders of Radio Veronica)**

As the deal between Joop van Ende (a leading TV producer in Holland whose programmes are now seen worldwide) Holland HitRadio and the Veronica organisation neared finalisation, Nozema began looking to improve the reach of the 828 signal on behalf of their new client, the reborn Radio Veronica.

Heinenoord upgrade

To be commercially viable, the station near Rotterdam needed to increase power but this would mean making its output directional. Normally two masts are used, but environmentalists demanded only one mast could be used.

NOZEMA (who operated almost all the Dutch radio and TV transmitters at that time) turned to Paul Rusling for a solution, who promised a directional pattern using only one one mast. By increasing the hieght of the mast to 300 feet and adding a sloper element would give a directional radiation pattern. Then, the power could then be increased to 20 kilowatts without causing interference to the other stations on the same frequency.

The antenna type used was called "a sloper". They are much used by radio amateurs and in use at several low power broadcast stations. Aerial tuning huts for Heinenoord were built in Hull and shipped to Rotterdam on the daily overnight ferry and within three weeks the station was on the air, with a sharply tuned null to the west (-13dBi) which protected the English stations, such as *Chiltern Radio* in Luton and *Radio Aire* further north in Leeds.

The site took on even more of a 'nautical flavour' when Rusling brought in a former colleague to help with the installation. Peter Chicago had been the key radio engineer at Radio Caroline for over twenty years, but that station was now off the air.

HitRadio1224 was now taking so much money that Nozema and its owners did not want it off the air for even one day, while the upgrade work went ahead. Peter and Paul had problems with some tuning work on the site as the 828 frequency was being used by a standby service of 10 kilowatts from Lopik, not far away. This caused some burning to fingers from the mast when tuning, so the work was switched to night time hours. Working under spotlights, they then became an attraction for hundreds of moths and mosquitoes and both suffered multiple bites.

The improved Heinenoord facility gave excellent coverage on 828AM using a new 20-kilowatt Harris transmitter. This was DX25U model; 'U' means it's upgradable to 50kW, should more power be necessary. It was set to automatically reduce power to 5 kilowatts at dusk each day, and gave superb coverage in the Randstad and well into the Flemish speaking part of Belgium.

Veronica launched their new station, **HitRadio Veronica,** on MW, Cable and satellite on 1st September 1995. That same day, the NOS launched its own classical music station, Hilversum 4; public broadcasters the world over always like to run a spoiler when they feel threatened!

The passing of the Communicator over to Veronica was marked by an event on board the ship and a big party in Hilversum. Here are Nico Volker and some of the Holland FM team on board, as 1224 became *Veronica HitRadio*.

Nico Volker (2nd left) leads the 1224 AM handover.

It was a day of great celebration in the Veronica family with people from all walks of radio and the music industry invited. The previous night had also been a big occasion, marking the 21 years anniversary of the death of the station Radio Veronica from the radio ship Norderney off the coast of Scheveningen. Now finally Veronica could be heard once again, across most of the Netherlands with a far more powerful service. And just to delight the older members of the Veronica family, 1224 was being transmitted from on board a radio ship!

The ship was now owned by the *Holland Media Group*, which was a newly formed business partnership of the Veronica Foundation and RTL Radio Tele Luxembourg. The new private Veronica organisation also launched several new stations, all badged with the Veronica brand.

As well as Veronica HitRadio, the HMG planned four other stations: a classical station (Conzertzender), an alternative music channel (Kink FM), an Oldies channel and a News service. The 'All News' station was eventually heard on the 1395 frequency, *Veronica News Radio*. This used a 10-kilowatt Phillips transmitter from the Lopik site. It later became *Business Nieuws Radio* on the FM band after taking over frequencies of another station.

The Phillips transmitter had originally been intended to be installed on the Communicator as a spare or 'back up' unit but Nozema managers did not consider it good practice to mix types of equipment, especially at remote sites. Also the Harris DX50 unit had a lot of built in redundancy meaning the station would not be put off the air if one module failed, but could carry on at only marginally reduced power.

Veronica HitRadio identified the 1224 AM station with a slogan, *De hits van gisteren en het beste van nu* which means *the hits of yesterday and the best of nowadays*. It was now fighting for radio ratings with the big boys of Dutch radio: Radio 10 and Hilversum 3. These were later joined by **Sky Radio** and **Radio 538** who successfully sued the Dutch Government for the rights to an FM licence as well as being heard in most Dutch homes on cable and via satellite.

Unico Glorie, MD of Veronica Hit Radio

The Veronica organisation already had their own weekly media magazine that enjoyed weekly sales of well over a million copies and were well placed to promote the new stations. Veronica HitRadio became one of the first in Europe to televise its breakfast programme; something that other stations, including BBC Radio One, later followed.

The additional media attention that Veronica drew meant that extra security fencing had to be erected at the Trintelhaven site. The small restaurant at the north side of the marina was often overwhelmed with business as people came to show their children this curious phenomena of a floating radio ship, although by now all the programmes came from the very plush studio centre in Hilversum with just a small crew of engineers on board the ship.

The big name DJs of Veronica could now be heard on 1224 AM, or Veronica HitRadio as it was now called. Among these were nationally known DJs such as Jeroen van Inkel, Robert Jensen and Edwin Evers who dominated the schedule, with Kas van Iersel, Rob Stenders and Martijn Krabbé also joining.

Kas began his career as a pirate DJ in The Hague, mainly for Radio Centraal. He then went to work in Belgium, Italy and the USA. Eventually his demo tape was accepted by TROS and he produced the Top 50 Show. After a period with the AVRO, Kas joined the *Voice of Peace*, a radio ship in the Mediterranean. He used the name Kas Collins there and worked with Radio Caroline stars such as Carl Kingston and Crispian St John. By the mid nineties Kas was back in Holland and he joined Veronica HitRadio in 1996.

Other DJs who broadcast regularly on Veronica HitRadio are Edwin Zoo, Martijn Krabbe and Robert Jenson, who hosted the *Escapades Evening* show.

For a time there was a museum of offshore radio on the Communicator. This was mainly made up from large display boards taken from the Omroep Museum in Hilversum. They showed each offshore station plus one real 'live' exhibit: the two CSI Transmitters still on board from the Laser days in the 1980s. The museum was run by Martin Verdoorn but was only open to the public for a short time; Saturday and Sunday afternoons in the *HitRadio 1224* days, late Spring 1995.

Martin Verdoorn in the museum

By 1998, Holland Media Groep had won a new licence for Veronica HitRadio to broadcast on the FM Band and decided to have a complete new rebranding of the station for the change from AM to FM. They decided to change the name again *Veronica FM* and wanted to now drop any trace of the old Medium Wave days. As they were no longer on MW it was decided to dispense with the ship, which had served them well for almost three years as a relay station on 1224 kHz..

The Veronica team worked hard to sell the MV Communicator on to NOZEMA. A shipbroker had valued the vessel at a very low price, due to the large amount of concrete ballast placed into the ship which was now very difficult to move. It reduced the options for the ship which was now a liability.

* UPDATE *Veronica HitRadio* was recently reborn as part of a bouquet of twelve online radio stations, run by the giant TALPA organisation from their HQ at Naarderpoort. The station was called various names when run by Sky, including *RTL FM*, *TMF Radio*, then *TMF HitRadio* and more recently it is once again *Veronica HitRadio*.

19. Q RADIO

Radio London was a radio station that broadcast over Dutch cable networks from a train in a siding in the town of Zutphen for most of the 1990s. It began in 1995 and its leader was Peter Jansen. The train was previously used as the personal conveyance of Erik Honecker, the former leader of East Germany from 1971 until the Berlin Wall fell.

The station's output consisted of 'world music' interspersed with old Radio London jingles. Dutch radio expert Herbert Visser describes the station sound: "The whole thing was very weird. You'd hear that lovely 'It's smooth sailing, with the highly successful sound of Wonderful Radio London' jingle and then Fela Kuti (a Nigerian singer) or someone else would sing in the vernacular from the inlands of Africa or the Brazilian jungle."

The special train of Eric Honecker (leader of East Germany for 20 years) brought to Zupten railway sidings where it served as the studios for RADIO LONDON and then Q-RADIO broadcasting from the Communicator.

There were claims of breach of copyright, as the name Radio London had been registered as a trademark by a company in London, and many had scratched their head wondering why a cable only radio station in the east of Holland was named after the British capital. Radio London's name was changed to Q Radio in 1998, when the licence to broadcast on 1224 AM was obtained.

A rental deal had been made with NOZEMA for the new station, Q Radio, to use their 50kW transmitter from the ship and the transmissions of Q Radio began emanating from there in January 1998, but the ship remained on the IJsselmeer, giving excellent reception over the northern part of the Netherlands.

Audience figures were very poor however as the station's identity was very confusing and the music the station played was totally unknown. That didn't seem to matter however, as Peter Jansen (that's him on the next page) and Q-Radio was being bankrolled by Eckhart Winze, a multimillionaire who described himself "a professional hippie." Eckhart died in 2008 having mainly invested in 'green projects" after making his fortune in computer technology in the 1980's. His investment firm continues Eckhart's work even today.

At the same time, Veronica Hitradio also relinquished their use of the 828 kHz AM frequency from the mast at Heinenoord. This facility was relicensed to SBS (Scandinavian Broadcasting Systems) for a while as CAZ. The following year the CAZ radio station was sold on to Arrow (a Classic Rock and Jazz music station based in The Hague) who used it for their programmes for about seven further years. It has now been closed down and the mast demolished.

Q Radio had guaranteed good reception in the Randstad and Brabant but without the 828 transmitter at Heinenoord, reception to the south was poor. The decision was taken to move the ship to a site near Almere and on 14th October 1998, she was slowly towed to a new anchorage in the Pampushaven near Almere, just east of Amsterdam. The ship was towed slowly because in the Autumn the water in the IJsselmeer is lower and the Communicator risked running aground.

Once the ship was at the new berth at Pampushaven, Unico Glorie, the Managing Director of the Holland Media Group, officially handed the ship over to Peter Jansen, the founder of Q-Radio, during a ceremony which was televised and shown on the TV news that evening.

Peter Jansen led a team of about twenty broadcasters at QRadio, many of them club DJs from Rotterdam and Amsterdam who knew the 'world music' that the station played. Many of the shows were from Indonesian and Surinamese DJs and some from Aruba. He was also responsible for publishing a new magazine bearing the radio station's name and for managing meetings with the other Q Radio shareholder(s).

The station continued to broadcast its programmes from the train formerly belonging to Eric Honecker, still located out in the railway siding at Zutphen.

**Peter Jansen, founder & MD
of Radio London and Q-Radio**

Programmes were relayed from the train to the ship the Communicator by satellite link, for broadcasting on AM 1224. They broadcast the address on the air as Q Radio, Postbus 151, 7200 AD Zutphen and used a local phone number of 0575 515514. This will have sounded a bit strange to many listeners as, in the Netherlands, most national radio stations broadcast from Hilversum or the immediate area, but Zutphen is over an hour's drive away, to the east of Amsterdam, in the province of Gelderland.

The programmes were almost the same as previous ones, when they were using the name Radio London. But now the station was being heard all over the Netherlands and into Germany and Denmark with a powerful 50 kW MW signal from the radio ship, Communicator. The listening figures for commercial broadcaster QRadio show a 0.0 (zero-point-zero) rating, but there is was an optimistic way of viewing this low rating. The station's director, Peter Jansen says "Our listeners are loyal, but do not report to such listening surveys in such numbers that it is worth mentioning them to media planners and advertisers."

The station's very low budget makes it too expensive to carry out outside broadcasts. It had a lot of idealistic aims; 'Q' was said to stand for Quality. The station later expanded into a converted American school.

"Although the ship has good recognition and admiration for its nostalgia and history, many employees here at QRadio are not very happy with their new workplace," said one of the disc jockeys. "It is on the banks of the IJsselmeer! This is the same as being in the middle of nowhere. How the hell can you meet guests for your radio show out in this no man's land?"

The move did produce a few more listeners and Q Radio's share of the listeners rose to almost 0.5% within a few months. The main reason for this was because at last, people could hear the station on an ordinary radio. Previously listeners had to find the station on cable, and reception was limited to homes. Now it could be heard in cars.

DJ on the air in the Radio London / Q-Radio train

In February 1999 Ronald van der Meijden, Chief Executive from the *Sun Radio* cultural station in Rotterdam joined the board of Q Radio. He had been tone of the programme leaders at Radio Monique in its days on the Ross Revenge when that ship was a neighbour of the Communicator. Ronald then moved into the music business working in record companies, especially RnB lables. He was by now well known as the main voice of Urban *Radio 40* and the R&B Mix Show *The Groove Party* and had left Sun Radio when its owner, Gerro Vonk (see Holland FM above) changed the format to a more commercial format to appeal to older listeners.

By 1999, the Communicator was only visited about every ten days, by a couple of engineers to refuel the generator (which was in a small cubicle on the bank of the haven). The programmes were all uplinked to the ship from the Radio London train at Zutphen.

Later that year, there were rumours that all was not well between the radio station and its multi-millionaire backer. Eckhart Wintzen was said to be concerned at the high costs of broadcasting an ethical and green radio station from a communist train using a transmitter on an expensive ship, needing lots of fuel to keep the Communicator's powerful transmitter running

In April 2000 a splinter group seemed to be forming called Q The Beat, with its own web site, but this seemed to be only a way to escape for the high debt mountain that was building up again on the Communicator.

The station tried to relaunch as *Colorful Radio* in 2000 on cable only. This was a radio project also run by Peter Jansen that had been in the making since 1994. Peter Jansen later became a board member of the *Ghetto Radio Trust* as well as the director of a TV film called *Noise is My Voice* and set up more radio outlets in several cities in Africa, including in Nairobi. He now lives in Groningen and works for a charity called *Media4Africa*. Colourful Radio was eventually taken over by the NOS public station Radio 2 and the frequencies used for the *Soul and Jazz* splinter operation.

Soon the company faced bankruptcy proceedings but even the court could not accurately discover how much debt there was, or indeed who was responsible for which piece of it. The main creditor of Q Radio was *RnR Communications*, which was part owned by Rob van der Vegt. He later became CEO of the successor station, Q The Beat. The registered company that operated Q Radio was based at an address in Laren, owned by the founder, Peter Jansen.

20. Q – THE BEAT

After Q Radio's financial disaster in the spring, there was a 'legal repackaging' of the company in the Dutch courts. The 1224 frequency was temporarily used for a 15 day Veronica memorial broadcast, but from the standby Pye transmitter at Lopik. Eventually Q transmissions from the Communicator began again with a full relaunch, identifying as *Q The Beat* on 10th of December 2000. A new programme format was announced as "a big new start for radio in the post-millennium years."

The companies behind Q The Beat were *The Beat Goes On bv*, and *Media Matters bv* but the funding for the project seemed come from the huge American conglomerate, *Clear Channel Communications*. This is now called *iHeart Radio* and runs around 1500 radio stations. Its London Chief Executive was Roger Parry, who had played a part in the first radio stations on the ship, Laser 730, later called Laser 558. Clear Channel also had a big interest in MOJO, the major concert promoter in the Netherlands.

Q The Beat 1224 programmes were aimed unashamedly at 13 to 19 year olds, especially young immigrants and their secondary target was 20-34 year olds. They styled the station as 'Urban, a mixture of hip-hop and RnB music.' Its main identification jingles sang about "The best in urban music." Programmes came from a studio in Hoofddorp and they had a very high reach among teenagers, particularly in Amsterdam where the signal was strong.

At its launch in 2000 Q The Beat made particular emphasis of how it was a station not just 'down with the kids' but also "out on the streets". For the launch period it commissioned a lot of street art, with outdoor floor graphics in high profile urban locations. Many were outside major railway stations such as in Rotterdam, Utrecht and Amsterdam at the Centraal Station. They claimed that this was "virgin territory, that no radio station in the Netherlands had ever used this method before."

The station also hired some big name presenters from the world of dance music, including Slam FM!'s top DJ, **Edith den Doosh** and NewDance Radio's **Eddie Cream**. Edith said she had made the switch because she had previously felt stifled at SlamFM!

(<u>NOTE</u> Slam FM! is now operated by RadioCorp Holdings, run by ex Radio Monique Radio 10 DJ / newsreader Herbert Visser)

"Previously the owner of Slam! (Soedesh Moerlie) and I made all the playlist and scheduling decisions, but the moves towards commercialisation took away everything, including the DJ's free choices," explained Edith. "I am a radio DJ and want people to hear good music; I do not just want to make myself heard, through a microphone."

Edith took a slot in the mid afternoon at Q The Beat and played the eternal adolescent DJ and together with **DJ Owja** could often be heard swearing on the air. Edith later joined Radio 538 and presented some overnight shows.

Eddie Cream (Keur) is a well known DJ in the Netherlands having originally joined Radio Caroline in 1979 as Sebastian Peters. He has worked as a voice over artist at TROS, and as a creative consultant developing formats to Talpa and TV10, plus many other broadcasters.

Eddie hosted the coveted breakfast show at Q The Beat for over a year, and he became one of the station's longest serving DJs. He left Q in August 2002 for a show on Yorin FM and until 2016 he was heard on Radio 538.

On Saturdays, RnB star **Snoop Dogg** had his own radio show on the station with some very unusual mixes. The talk was very much fashion-led with a lot of discussion and comments about Snoop Dogg's new range of clothes for sale.

Q The Beat was certainly turning a few heads, but seems that the ears did not tune in for very long. One of the Netherland's oldest broadcasters VPRO (it is a liberal Protestant organisation) sent a camera crew to the station to make a programme about this latest radio station from the Communicator; it was shown as part of the 'Seven Days' series in March 2001. It included interviews with Mijneer van der Vegt, Nicolet Don, the station's lawyer, and Leontien van der Meer, the accountant of Radio Matters BV and Q The Beat.

Rob van der Vegt was the Managing Director of the new station. He said that, because they played a lot of rap and hip hop music; maybe it wasn't so out of place on a medium better known today for talk radio (medium wave). "Ideally we would like obviously one FM frequency for the whole country," said Mr van der Vegt. "We must wait and see whether we will succeed.

"We are a strong supporter of the auction method because it is the most transparent distribution method," said Rob. "How incumbent commercial broadcasters react to this is exactly the attitude that they accused the former public broadcasters of. However, we're not worried. Our owners, Clear Channel, owns more than a thousand radio stations. The necessary funds are available when they are required."

The station began campaigning politically for the VVV (a conservative party), whose belief was that the fairest option for radio was to start frequency allocations again and give every organisation an equal chance to broadcast.

At Easter 2001, Q The Beat started relaying its programmes on FM in Alkmaar, using an educational station taken over by Media Matters bv, one of the owners of Q The Beat. They used a frequency previously licensed to Happy Radio, with the FM outlet simply rebroadcasting the signal received from the AM transmitter on the Communicator.

None of Q The Beat's programmes originated on the ship however, which was used simply as a relay transmitter base. The programmes always came from a studio in Hoofddorp, at the end of the Schiphol runways. Despite its Urban format, the station pre-tested all its music and introduced a new jingle package almost monthly. The walls of the studio were adorned with the slogan *Radio paints pictures that no one can put on the screen.*

The emphasis on street art and such slogans made many radio traditionalists wonder whether the team behind Q The Beat realised that this was radio, a medium that works better with other senses than vision?

MD Rob van der Vegt seemed to be very aware of what makes radio succeed when he said: "1224 AM is an easy nationwide airwave frequency to communicate and this is one of the most essential things in radio. The air still provides the most effective distribution option."

Promising words, but he soon seems to have forgotten them and wanted to drop the station's 'single frequency'in for a mixture of FM frequencies.

Q The Beat MD Rob van der Vegt

At the end of March 2001, Q The Beat began broadcasting messages every hour asking its listeners to bombard the Ministry of Verkeer en Waterstaat with requests for Q The Beat to be given FM frequencies. The station was proposing to partner *Arrow Classic Rock*, whose directors were also asking to move to the FM band. The Ministry had asked stations for patience pending a new round of frequency awards, but many of the big FM stations were trading their frequencies for cash.

A major event for Q The Beat was a large music festival for fans of urban music called the *Megafestijn*. It was held in the Jaarbeurs in Utrecht during July 2001, when over 75,000 signatures were collected supporting the station's request for an FM outlet. The station was now claiming that its target audience of teenagers generally did not use the MW band. "Our station's audience would feel more comfortable with an FM station," they said. "This will make Q The Beat even more successful." At this time the station was attracting only 0.5% of the Dutch radio audience.

Rob van der Vegt from Amersfoort, the CEO of the station, argued that "Our station has millions invested which we did on the basis of tough political decisions and promises of the government. Now is the time for promises made by politicians to be honoured," he said. "We accuse the (broadcasting) committee of having an irresponsible plan. This is proven by the fact that *Business Nieuws Radio* moved to another frequency, simply because they might not have sufficient financial resources." He accused BNR of wrongly taking FM frequencies, (in parallel with 1395AM from Trintelhaven) which had originally been assigned to JFK for a 24-hour jazz format.

Eventually the Government decided to cancel the frequency auction and instead charge all the existing stations a combined licence fee of 15 million.

By the autumn of 2002, the Communicator was looking 'the worse for wear' after a couple of harsh winters. She was a very lonely and a very forlorn sight with the red, white and blue paintwork peeling. Plans to repaint the ship were made however, environmental reasons demanded she move to a sealed dock for the work, which would be expensive. So the Communicator retained her red, white and blue facepaint, made for Holland FM, however there had been a change in her colours on the IJselmeer that few noticed. Originally her bows were red and the stern was blue, with a white 'midriff'. These were then swapped with the bows becoming blue and the stern painted red. The Holland FM name on the ship's stern was painted out and simply a '1224' number applied to the bows, as usually seen on warships.

Towards the end of 2001, Q TheBeat began playing more and more non stop music, dropping the programmes of almost all its DJs. An official statement from the station claimed that they had only taken the 1224 AM frequency as temporary measure, to test their music format, and really wanted to be on FM. At the same time, Q TheBeat acquired an extra frequency, 1557 AM in Amsterdam, where it was rumoured to be launching a rural radio station, however that plan did not materialise.

Q The Beat made two applications to the Dutch authorities for an FM transmitter while still transmitting on 1224 kHz from the Communicator. One of their business plans showed a turnover of 160 million Guilders.

Clear Channel Communications, which was providing almost all the funding for the station then decided to abandon its quest for a licence and sold its share. It had taken a long time before the auction began, leading to legal procedures by Q and others to speed this up, but Q TheBeat never managed to win an FM licence. Most months, the costs of renting the transmitter on board the ship from NOZEMA were exceeding the station's income.

During the Autumn of 2002, Q The Beat failed to pay many of its bills, including the rental for the transmitter and to another contractor who provided power from generators located on the dyke. By December 2002, the fuel level was running low but the paymasters, Clear Channel Communications, did not want to pay any longer. The station simply died when the last drops of fuel were used. The last day of broadcasting was 10th of December 2002, exactly two years to the day since Q The Beat had started broadcasting. The Communicator's powerful 50kW transmitter had sent out its last broadcast on 1224 kHz.

The 1224 frequency which had covered the Netherlands so well thanks to the powerful transmitter on the MV Communicator was later licensed to *Quality Radio bv*, not connected to Peter Jansen's Q-Radio. Quality Radio is a company run by Dutch radio entrepreneur Ruud Poeze. He also holds licences for several other MW frequencies in the Netherlands.

The 1224 frequency is still in use as a 'gap filler' for Radio Paradijs in Utrecht but Mr Poeze is in danger of losing this in 2017. In 2016, Mr Poeze fought the Dutch Government in the Rotterdam High Court to prevent them licensing further very low power transmitters on 747 kHz.

Early in 2003 NOZEMA removed the Harris DX50 transmitter and it was installed at their AM site on Flevopolder.

The mooring at Almere was quite remote and there were now children or vandals living nearby and the ship became a frequent target for attempts to plunder it for equipment and just for mindless vandalism. "It was basically being raped and pillaged while at the Pampushaven," commented one engineer.

There were already moves to buy the now silent MV Communicator and several interested parties visited her during the first half of 2003 at Pampushaven.

Among these was Ray Anderson who had bought her in 1986 from the Admiralty Marshall. Ray had been renting air time on the 1395 frequency from Trintelhaven for another station called **Radio London** and **Big L**, which he hoped could serve the UK from Holland. He was prevented from using the Radio London name by the threats of legal action from other radio enthusiasts, who in turn were sued by the BBC in 2015 over use of the Radio london name.

The 1395 transmitter at Trintelhaven could only be heard along the east coast of the UK and so did not prove commercially viable, although it attracted a cult listenership. Big L continues today online with a small but enthusiastic core of listeners to its online service.

The radio ship was now owned by Rob van der Vegt, acting on behalf of Clear Channel, who had bids to buy it from other potential owners. NOZEMA were happy to help introduce Mr van der Vegt to a stream of interested buyers who made the journey to her Pampushaven berth in the coldest winter the Netherlands had experienced for some years.

There were however some concerns about asbestos in the ship, which might be an expensive liability when the ship finally came to be scrapped. Among the offers to buy the ship were one of €10,000 from Ruud Poeze, who won the 1224 licence in 2003. He offered to hire the ship at Almere from the owners, but they were keen to move it on and would not rent it out.

A deal was eventually done with a British consortium who eventually bought the Communicator for only €5,000. The new buyer was to be a project headed by Dave Miller and Janie Ash. They planned for the Communicator to move to the UK and be refitted for "The Super Station."

NOTE Belgian company Persgroep used the name *QMusic*, for a new radio station, using the frequencies of *Radio Noordzee Nationaal*. It was nothing to do with Q TheBeat and did not come from the Communicator. Subsequently QMusic became a leading radio station in The Netherlands.

Part 3 - Scuppered in Scapa Flow

21.   THE SUPER STATION

In March 2003 the sale of the ship was completed and her ownership transferred to The Super Station, an ethical radio group, run by Manchester radio DJ Dave Miller, and his partner Janie Ash. They had consulted with Paul Rusling and others for some months on buying the vessel and wanted to bring it back to the UK. The ship was to play a crucial role in their plans to create a new genre of radio station in 2004.

Dave is a well-known in the DJ world having worked for many radio stations, while Janie is a radio sales executive who had worked with Dave at City Beat in Northern Ireland.

David began his love affair with radio on *Radio Caroline*, joining the ship in July 1988 when he was only seventeen years old. He then got a job at *Radio City* in Liverpool and was later heard on *BRMB* in Birmingham, *Key 103* Manchester and *Rock FM* in Preston. Dave was the launch Programme Controller at *City Beat* in Belfast, hiring such radio legends as Stephen Nolan, Kenny Tosh, Christine Bleakley and Lisa Flavelle.

While working on Radio Caroline in summer 1987, the Ross Revenge, Dave became enchanted and beguilled by the neighbouring ship, the MV Communicator.

His colleagues on Radio Caroline told him of all the fun and excitement that had accompanied her every move. She was silent at that time but Dave had become smitten; he was very determined to do something with her.

The Super Station Founders: Dave Miller & Janie Ash

During Spring 2003 the Communicator had been extensively vandalised with severe damage being caused to the remaining electronics equipment, the equipment in the ship's wheelhouse and to many of the Communicator's portholes.

The financial deal to purchase the Communicator was completed in June 2003 and on the 24th, Dave had the ship towed from Almere back to IJmuiden harbour on the North Sea coast by an *Iskes Tug Company* vessel. Despite it being a warm midsummer day, there were no crowds to watch her sail past the back of Amsterdam's Centraal station.

A few days after she arrived in IJmuiden, someone crept on board one night and opened two of the seacocks on the ship. This allowed water in and soon the ship was listing, quite badly. A police investigation ensued and many local vandals interviewed but no culprit was ever brought to justice.

Communicator sinking in IJmuiden harbour

Dave and Janie quickly ensured the ship was pumped dry and undertook the essential work needed to restore the ship to good order. The large windows that had been cut in the side of the ship during the Holland FM days had to be welded closed for her sea voyage. This meant using large steel plates to comply with insurance demands. Despite these costly setbacks, Dave and Janie were undeterred and both were driven by a passion and determination to restore the Communicator to her former glory.

Joining the Super Station project in Holland was Martin Gilbert, a former BT engineer. He knew the ship well, having accompanied Paul Rusling to one of the balloon tests in early 1984. Gilbert had now moved to the Orkney Islands, which were about to become a major milestone in the ship's life.

On the 19th December 2003, the JWR Apollo towed the MV Communicator across the North Sea back to the UK. It was an uneventful crossing for the fifty-year-old tug, almost as old as the MV Communicator. She made a steady ten knots to Lowestoft, the port where Paul Rusling and Paul Hodge had bought the ship, just over twenty years before. The Communicator was home for one final visit.

Lowestoft was the home port of Gardline Shipping, whose Chairman George Darling had once said that he expected to welcome 'The Seeker' back to his fleet eventually. Her relaunch as *Laser Hot Hits* had stopped that. The Super Station were hoping to collect some spare parts and draw on the expertise of former crew members.

The Super Station had decided to have an office on Madison Avenue, just as had Laser in the 1980s. Dave chose an address just along the street at number 305, a few blocks down from the original palatial offices. This was the third address that stations from the ship had on Madison Avenue, moving from 341 to 515 and finally to 305.

The Super Station's plan was to moor the Communicator off the coast of County Dublin and broadcast from there. A key part of the project's finance was withdrawn and the team realised that the weather at that location would probably be too uncomfortable for the crew of the ship, so a new location was sought.

The Super Station's Managing Director, Dave Miller, said that he was "jubilant that Phase One of the project is complete and the ship is home where she belongs. I am passionate about the Communicator and about my vision for radio in the 21st century. I can't reveal any more details about the project at this stage, but can say that what we want to do with the ship is going to be innovative, exciting and fresh."

Janie Ash, the Super Station project's Chief Executive was equally passionate about the company that she had co-founded with Mr Miller: "Our journey so far is a testament to our determination to make this project work. We are committed to building a profitable and happy company," said Janie. "We are very focussed and clear in our vision and the key to it all is the MV Communicator, our most valuable asset," she continued. "Our journey has been nothing short of miraculous and the future is extremely bright. What we have here is a new paradigm for business in the 21st century."

The Communicator had come home for Christmas and was soon the centre of attention. She was visited by many of her former crewmembers, engineers and disc jockeys alike, and no small number of former listeners to Laser too, all eager to see the ship once again and find out what the plans were being made for her future. The skeleton crew of the vessel erected a Christmas Tree on the wheelhouse roof (see picture on the left) and a couple of quite enjoyable parties were held on board even though the ship still had no heating working.

The ship received many visitors over that Christmas and New Year holiday period, with many former staff, crew and even some of her old neighbours from Radio Caroline too were seen clambering all over the ship.

Opinions were divided as to whether she looked worse now than when she first sailed in back in the 1980s, although most were agreed that she had been a lot better cared for during her years in the Netherlands. They seemed to ignore the vandalism of the past year and the effects of a few feet of water that had been allowed in while in Ijmuiden.

Even her old fans, the DTI, came along to check on her readiness for sea and set up an observation base in the harbour with two men assigned to keep an eye on the Super Station team. They logged everyone on and off the boat for several weeks with high powered cameras equipped with telefoto lenses and ran checks on dozens of cars visiting that showed any interest in the ship.

A considerable amount of renovation work was done while she was in Lowestoft by Paul and Roy, the Balls Brothers. They are two well known radio enthusiasts who live in East Anglia and who moved onto the Communicator for several weeks during the restoration work. Other helpers were recruited by the Super Station to their cause and the ship was slowly brought back into a state where she could be lived in. The mess was no longer a total mess and had plush red velour seating fitted. The ship's equipment also had some restoration work done, but no competent engineer was available to work on the main engine and get that fully serviceable.

The domestic quarters were also given a very good overhaul as these had been neglected for the ten years that the ship had not been 'lived in'. Since the Holland FM days at Trintelhaven she had been a remote unattended relay transmitter. The galley was completely refitted, the production areas tidied up and redecorated and some heating to cabins was restored.

The walls were stripped and made good, new carpets laid and equipment installed to make life for her crew as comfortable as possible. Plush red velour seat pads were added in major reupholstery.

The crews did sterling work despite limited funding. Their only problem seems to have been adjusting the mooring ropes, an important job as the tide in Lowestoft harbour rose and fell twice a day.

Portside messroom seating restored

Life in Lowestoft soon became too difficult with the British Authorities getting concerned at the plans for the ship. They were not convinced that Ireland was ever the intended destination and suspected that the ship might about to anchor off East Anglia and broadcast to London once again.

The Communicator finally left Lowestoft on Saturday 21st August towed by the tug Goliath. It was a big disappointment for her fans to see her dragged along the coast.

The Communicator was now in her twenty first year as a radio ship and many guessed this could be her final voyage. When she had left Lowestoft in August 1983 bound for Florida and refitting as a radio ship she had been under her own power and fully crewed; now she was under tow, with portholes sealed closed and an uncertain fate.

The Communicator leaves Lowestoft

Her destination was St Margaret's Hope on South Ronaldsay in the Orkney Islands where she arrived three days later. She still carried the red, white and blue colours applied for her broadcasts of *Holland FM* in 1994. She flew the Dutch flag still and her port of registry was still Rotterdam

The Orkney Islands are a sparsely populated part of Scotland, just 20,000 souls and almost half of them living in Kirkwall which is some distance from St Margaret's Hope. Lying at the southern end of Scapa Flow, where the ship was to be moored, SMH is a small port with just a short pier at the southern end of Scapa Flow, quite difficult to reach from the main Orkney Island and two main centres of population (Kirkwall and Stromness) but this made security much less of a nightmare. The pier was just 15 nautical miles from the Scottish mainland at Gill's Bay, just to the east of Thurso (Scrabster).

The Pier at St Margaret's Hope also serves Pentland Ferries, a family business owned by Andrew Banks OBE and his wife Susan. In 2004, when the Super Station launched, Andrew had the well known vessel the MV Claymore in service on the route and the Communicator was often photographed lying alongside her. The Claymore has since been replaced by a sleek new catamaran, the MV Pentalina, providing a link to the mainland in less than an hour.

A UK 'Restricted Service Licence' was obtained from OFCOM, the UK broadcasting regulator, enabling the station to broadcast on FM for the three months from September to November .

Martin Gilbert had moved to the Orkneys the previous year having run an RSL station at Montrose in mainland Scotland. He suggested that Orkney was ripe for commercial radio so Dave Miller and Janie Ash took a trip over to the Islands. They agreed that and felt a three months trial could work. The moorings in Lowestoft were very expensive and St Margaret's Hope Pier Trust was keen to have the MV Communicator there.

In advance of the Communicator's arrival at St Margaret's Hope, Gilbert was tasked with making some arrangements at the FM transmitter site. This was one of the highest locations, close to Kirkwall, the Island's capital. When Martin asked for the key to the site, the landlord requested £600 rental due for the period which Gilbert refused to pay.

The station was late in getting on the air due to 'problems with the link receiver that was to carry programmes from the ship up to the transmitter. Replacement equipment had to be flown in from *Broadcast Warehouse* in London to get the station launched.

It was the 11th September before programmes started as the ship had arrived without some of the necessary electronic equipment. The first test signals were simply online however eventually the FM signal, on 105.4 appeared. At first it was quite weak and in mono but the signal was soon in stereo and a lot stronger, being heard over the Orkneys, although some tests were heard over the Internet feed.

Two experienced female presenters, Dee Kelly from the USA and Tiiu Shelley from Canada, had been hired to present programmes on the Super Station. Hiring them won the station a lot of advance publicity in the local 'Orcadian' newspaper. They were to be the mainstay of the station's broadcasts, with Julian Hodgkiss, a good friend of Dave Miller, being appointed Station Manager and heading up the breakfast show.

MD Julian Hodkiss.

Julian had previously launched Tower FM and Dee 106.3 in the North West and later became station manager at Fresh Radio in North Yorkshire. The music choice was HOT Adult Contemporary, aimed at a wide age group.

Dee Keely was the first voice on the air and formally launched the station at 10am. The second lady on the air for the Super Station was Tiiu Shelley, who comes from Bonavista in Newfoundland and who studied at Senea College.

She has worked for several radio stations, beginning her broadcasting career as a volunteer at City TV and then a radio station called CFRB in Toronto. Tiiu worked at the CN Radio group as a freelance broadcaster and then took a job at Lancashire radio station, *107 The Bee* as a Sales Consultant, before joining *Fresh Radio* in North Yorkshire. Tiiu then took a job at Lancashire radio station, *107 The Bee* as a Sales Consultant, before joining *Fresh Radio* in North Yorkshire. She did a few stints out in the Middle East on *Mood Radio* in Amman and now lives in Skipton where she works in PR.

Tiiu Shelley

The reaction from listeners was incredible, and the Super Station became an overnight success across Orkney, while the DJs became minor celebrities throughout the islands. Dave Miller was delighted that his hard work was finally starting to pay off, despite the huge challenges and expense involved in the upkeep and maintenance of the Communicator. The team all lived in the Murray Arms Hotel in St Margaret's Hope for the entire trial period.

The Super Station's editorial area not only included the Orkney Islands but also Caithness on the Scottish mainland where it would be clearly heard. For a while towards the end of 2008 the station attracted a cult following in and around Caithness, despite an opt-out ILR relay operating there called *Caithness FM*. There was considerable local support and discussion of the station in the local press.

For the FM transmissions, the Super Station used a Broadcast Warehouse transmitter on 105.4 installed at the Wideford Hill site, owned by the SSE, also known as the Hydro Board. It was well over five hundred feet ASL, overlooking the Bay ''Firth and Scapa Flow. The site got a better signal down into Kirkwall, the capital of the Orkneys, than could be achieved from the ship out at St Margaret's Hope.

The equipment used by the Super Station included an Orban 'Optimod' audio processor and a stereo spatial enhancer. The equipment was all maintained by George Flett, who was the RF engineer during the Super Station's first broadcasts, from the Communicator in 2004 and for the subsequent full licence period. George was a very experienced radio amateur who lived locally and stayed with the station to the very end, performing a lot of extra duties.

The Super Station's remit was to offer a broad range of popular and contemporary music. It also broadcast local news bulletins on the half hour and national news from Sky Radio at the top of the hour.

The company also ran a radio presenter training school and had several well-known radio names among its team, including Ryan Woodman, Gary King and Peter Quinn, all with experience on other ship-borne radio stations such as Radio Caroline or the Voice of Peace. Other disc jockeys heard on the SuperStation included Paul Hollins, Sean Coleman and Will Atkinson, as well as Sam Turner, Andy Lawson, Ron Brown and JC.

Super Station DJ Gary King

The Super Station made its final transmissions from the Communicator at 7pm on the 23rd of November 2004. Twenty one years before she had been en route from Florida to the Azores with a full crew of seamen and six excited DJs, ethusiastically setting out on the adventure of a lifetime in Europe. Now the MV Communicator was to be left silent and cold on the edge of a scrapyard without even a lone harbour generator set running. A sad fate for a ship that had meant so much to so many.

Despite the huge personal love that Dave Miller had for radio ships, he had now begun to realise that the upkeep of the ship was too much of a burden for a local radio station to sustain. He reluctantly put the MV Communicator up for sale in December 2004 for just £25,000 and announced that the Super Station was seeking a base on land from which to broadcast.

The end of transmissions from the Communicator was not the end of Super Station, which went on to many more years serving the Orkney Islands. The Super Station used the RSL transmissions from the Communicator to support their bid for a Community Radio licence for Orkney. This was eventually awarded by OFCOM in September 2005 but it was to be late 2007 before test transmissions could commence.

When the station was formally launched in January 2008, programmes no longer came from the Communicator but from a new base in the Islands' capital, Kirkwall. The studios at 39 Junction Road were modest by ILR standards but did boast two phone numbers: 01856 877552 and 877559, which would usually by answered by whoever was on the air at the time. Most of the Super Station's broadcast team were volunteers and it was often a struggle to pay the rent and utilities.

The station later used a studio at The Old Hospital in Kirkwall. They had promised 20% speech in their Licence Application and to include local and Celtic music, however very little was every played and the station presenters seemed at their happiest when spinning their favourite Top 40 hits.

Graham Brown is a former Press Officer for the BBC and a print journalist, but has never worked in radio. He blogs about the local media and on his blog he said: "The Super Station has lively pop music shows and gives local businesses a chance to advertise on the radio. The presenters, and the music played, could be almost anywhere in the UK."

While fondly remembered by many Orcadians, the station suffered from the recession at its launch and was not the resounding financial success it had been during the trial broadcasts from the Communicator in 2004. Dave Miller and the Programme Director **Ryan Woodman** built a viable and successful station which ran for seven years, providing Orkney with its only dedicated radio station.

Ryan had been working at Radio Caroline, where he was involved in negotiating for carriage on SKY and also worked with Chris Cary for a while on his 'Cow' venture in Australia

When the Super Station took on Ryan, founder Dave Miller said "Ryan is only 23 and while I have worked with some of the best programmers in the country in my career but never have I worked with someone as loyal and talented as this. Obviously to have such an asset in somewhere as remote as Orkney is superb. Big groups are already asking about him however this is our way of showing our appreciation for his commitment and it means that Ryan will always be part of the decision making for the project."

Dave Miller and his team persevered with the station for almost 7 years, with Super Station both on the FM transmitter and online. It finally closed down on 16th November, 2014. "Despite our love for the Super Station and our belief in serving the people of Orkney, the business was no longer viable, due to a lack of public funding and dwindling advertising revenue," said Dave Miller.

Following the closure of the Super Station, Ryan Woodman moved to various stations in the Manchester area, including SILK FM in Macclesfield and Dave Miller moved to Dublin to launch a new radio station.

A Manx lifeline?
The Communicator's last chance to broadcast seemed to come from the *Isle of Man International Broadcasting Plc*, a company with a licence to broadcast on 279 kHz Long Wave with up to 500,000 watts. Their *Musicman 279* station would have covered the entire British Isles and Ireland as well as some of the near continent. It had recently had an appeal to build a transmitter on land, but it had obtained permission to anchor a radio ship within Manx territorial waters and transmit from there. This was to be a 'stop gap' measure for a year while a more permanent installation built on a man made island (to be have been called *Caroline Island*) was installed in Ramsey Bay. Talks were held with Dave Miller to buy the Communicator and the vessel secured by paying him a £7,500 deposit for the ship.

IMIB's Marine Superintendent, Captain James Connolly, flew from the Isle of Man to Orkney to inspect the vessel however what he found was not encouraging. Virtually all the ship's paperwork was missing and there were still tidemarks evident from the IJmuisden flooding escapade.

She would need dry-docking and considerable work as well as bringing up to date with the latest SOLAS (Safety of Life at Sea) requirements. Around £160,000 would need investing to make the ship properly seaworthy and serviceable; the IMIB board decided to look elsewhere for a platform for their transmitter.

The Musicman project foundered in 2006 after disagreements within its board over the company's share structure. Directors who had invested over £2 million to secure the licence and fight a legal battle over planning problems were reluctant to give a shareholding of more than 25% to new investors who would provide the funds to launch the station. The professionals left the company in 2006.

Dave Miller was very keen to sell the ship and announced that he would accept any reasonable offer for her. Late in 2005 the Communicator again began listing and it was found that the 'repaired' seacock that had been vandalised in IJmuiden was once again letting in water. The ship was hurriedly beached by a scratch crew from Pentland Ferries around the far side of the pier at St Margaret's Hope in the hope of stopping more water coming in.

At one stage in late 2006 the UK Government sent two investigators up to Kirkwall to check that the equipment wasn't being transferred to a new radio ship. They had been fed rumours that a splinter group of Radio Caroline funded by Chris Cary were planning to fit out a ship with parts from the Communicator.

The group bought a fifty kilowatt Telefunken transmitter in Germany that sat in a container on Mr Cary's driveway all ready for use. The TRAM transmitter was later revealed to have been purchased for use by Cary and Rusling in a breakaway project from the IMIB company in the Isle of Man.

That station was fully licensed to transmit from a ship anchored in Manx waters but they confirmed that they would not be using the Communicator.

50 kW transmitter on Chris Cary's drive

Eventually Dave Miller accepted the princely sum of £1,000 from the owner of Pentland Ferries in Orkney and she remained on site in St Margaret's Hope at the quay for a couple more years. In 2007 radio enthusiasts were still talking about making offers to buy the ship, either to convert her into a museum or perhaps sailed to a more accessible port in England. Several enquiries were received by Pentland Ferries, the new owners of the ship, but many of those enquiring never even made the trip to visit the vessel.

The main ship's engine was almost sold for £20,000 to a Greek shipping company. They needed precisely that model to replace the main engine in one of their ships that had done seven times as many hours as that on the Communicator. The radio ship's engine had only been sparingly used for the last 22 years, however the logistics of removing it from the Communicator proved too complex and financially prohibitive.

The ship's transmitting mast was taken down in early summer 2007 having lasted thirteen years but it took the new Orcadian owners over three years to manually strip the main structure of the ship down to the keel. The scrappers tore the side plates out, carefully removing her key components, such as the generators and by late 2009 all that was left was the aft structure and the shell of the engine room.

No fewer than eleven radio stations had broadcast from the ship, some completely self contained, some using the ship as a relay base. Some of those stations had been at low power and covered a very small area and some with a full fifty thousand watts of power that were regularly heard in several countries. Some of the stations had lasted only a few days, most of them had broadcast for more than six months. One however managed almost three years on the air, only leaving when it got access to an FM network. During that station's time transmitting from the Communicator, it turned over about 15 million Guilders, over £6 million sterling.

And so the ship ended her days being dismantled where she lay in Scapa Flow. It was a very sad end to a ship that brought so much happiness and joy, not to mention fun and excitement, to millions of radio listeners down the years, especially those in the UK and in the Netherlands.

Some Laser souvenirs are still available
Including historical recordings, jingles and T-shirts, etc:
(See *http://worldofradio.co.uk/Laser.html*)

by Paul Alexander Rusling

EULOGY TO A FRIEND

She was a strong little ship, home to many a brave seamen, engineers and disc jockeys. The gallant men and women who served aboard her each deserve a special 'Thank You' for all their time and efforts and for all the long hours, often for little reward, that they unselfishly dedicated to the cause of radio.

Thanks should also go to the many suppliers and not forgetting those who also served and helped in many other ways, whether by active assistance or simply by turning a blind eye. We thank and salute you all.

The Communicator at her final berth
Her best ever mast, still standing, proud and erect.

Goodbye dear old Communicator,
May you forever float in our thoughts.

ABOUT THE AUTHOR

Paul Rusling learned radio engineering at college in Hull. As no grants were available he paid his fees and living expanses by working as disc jockey in night clubs In 1973 he joined Radio Caroline as a disc jockey and hosted the station's breakfast programme. He and his wife Anne managed nightclubs and pubs and eventually settled down to raise a family at the Punch Tavern in Whitstable in Kent. It was while based there that he began working on converting the Communicator for its use as a floating radio station, her role for the next 21 years.

He switched his attentions to several other projects as a broadcast consultant and has since been involved in 18 successful licence applications, mostly for large scale national radio stations. His work has included programming, engineering and management functions and has taken him to many other countries across Europe and the Middle East.

Paul has written for many publications and magazines and has also written several books on radio. His most recent work describes how to build and operate an online radio station, *Internet Radio 2016*. That book is available as a regular book or can be downloaded as a Kindle or eBook, at

http://worldofradio.co.uk

Paul is also involved with a broadcast consultancy, WBC, which assists radio stations to solve their problems. WBC has several engineers with offshore broadcasting expertise available for similar unusual projects. WBC's expert

maritime lawyers ensure the team and their clients stay on the right of the law. While nothing at sea is cheap, neither is it necessary to win the lottery to have your own radio station on a ship, but if you think the prices charged by professionals are expensive, be warned – amateurs can cost even more!

WBC's web site can be found
at **http://worldwidebroadcast.co**

How to build, launch and operate
Your own online radio station

We are on the cusp of a huge expansion of online radio;
from 100,000 stations today to millions in the next few years.

Internet Radio 2016

This is a comprehensive guide to building and launching your own online radio station, written by international radio consultant, Paul Rusling

While traditional broadcasting via the ether has continued to thrive, the use of the internet to carry radio and TV programmes to the global audience has recently exploded. This is largely due to the medium of Internet streaming being free of government licensing.

Would-be broadcasters need only comply with legal requirements regarding libel and pay copyright fees for any commercial music they broadcast.

YOU could be the next radio sensation and turn your hobby into a fun business. This book will guide you though the procedures, advise you on the equipment and tell you how to stream your programmes though the Internet.

AVAILABLE NOW
Immediate despatch
via Amazon
This 280 page book could be
on your doormat in the morning!

Details via this link
http://amzn.to/2dGslad

or as an E-Book
Download NOW
for reading on
your **Kindle**
or computer
mobile phone
or tablet
http://amzn.to/2cO9e2H